Copyright © 2023 by Bonnie Heller. All rights reserved.

No part of this publication may be reproduced, distributed, or transmitted in any form or by any means, including photocopying, recording, or other electronic or mechanical methods, without the prior written permission of the publisher, except in the case of brief quotations embodied in critical reviews and certain other noncommercial uses permitted by copyright law.

Disclaimer

The information provided within this book is for general informational purposes only. While the author has taken every effort to provide accurate and current information, the places, experiences, and practicalities of travel can change rapidly and thus the author makes no representation or warranty of any kind, express or implied, regarding the accuracy, adequacy, validity, reliability, availability, or completeness of any information in this book.

Neither the author nor the publisher will be liable for any errors or omissions in this information nor for the availability of this information. The author and publisher will not be liable for any losses, injuries, or damages from the display or use of this information.

Readers are encouraged to verify any information from this book before making any decision or taking any action. The author and publisher disclaim any and all liability resulting from the interpretation and use of the information contained in this book.

CONTENTS

1. GIRONA, SPAIN 1
2. WROCLAW, POLAND 3
3. PORTO, PORTUGAL 5
4. GHENT, BELGIUM 7
5. TIMISOARA, ROMANIA 10
6. TRIESTE, ITALY 12
7. RIGA, LATVIA 14
8. LILLE, FRANCE 16
9. GOTHENBURG, SWEDEN 18
10. NANTES, FRANCE 20
11. PLOVDIV, BULGARIA 22
12. VALENCIA, SPAIN 24
13. UTRECHT, NETHERLANDS 26
14. SARAJEVO, BOSNIA AND HERZEGOVINA 28
15. KRAKOW, POLAND 30
16. VILNIUS, LITHUANIA 32
17. BOLOGNA, ITALY 34
18. TOULOUSE, FRANCE 36
19. CLUJ-NAPOCA, ROMANIA 38
20. INNSBRUCK, AUSTRIA 40
21. BRUGES, BELGIUM 42
22. HELSINKI, FINLAND 44
23. TARTU, ESTONIA 46
24. LJUBLJANA, SLOVENIA 48
25. KAZAN, RUSSIA 51
26. SPLIT, CROATIA 53

27.	GRONINGEN, NETHERLANDS	55
28.	STRASBOURG, FRANCE	57
29.	NICOSIA, CYPRUS	59
30.	BERGEN, NORWAY	61
31.	LUXEMBOURG CITY, LUXEMBOURG	63
32.	VIGO, SPAIN	65
33.	KAUNAS, LITHUANIA	67
34.	BRISTOL, ENGLAND	69
35.	SALZBURG, AUSTRIA	71
36.	CÓRDOBA, SPAIN	73
37.	ZAGREB, CROATIA	75
38.	TURKU, FINLAND	77
39.	AALBORG, DENMARK	79
40.	GAZIANTEP, TURKEY	81
41.	BERN, SWITZERLAND	83
42.	NOVI SAD, SERBIA	85
43.	STIRLING, SCOTLAND	87
44.	BILBAO, SPAIN	88
45.	BANJA LUKA, BOSNIA AND HERZEGOVINA	90
46.	STAVANGER, NORWAY	92
47.	GRAZ, AUSTRIA	94
48.	ODENSE, DENMARK	96
49.	LINZ, AUSTRIA	98
50.	VARNA, BULGARIA	100
51.	LEEUWARDEN, NETHERLANDS	102
52.	BRNO, CZECH REPUBLIC	103
53.	GENOA, ITALY	106
54.	ELCHE, SPAIN	107

55. NEWCASTLE UPON TYNE, ENGLAND 109
56. PULA, CROATIA 111
57. TAMPERE, FINLAND 113
58. HELSINGBORG, SWEDEN 115
59. BATH, ENGLAND 117
60. ESKISEHIR, TURKEY 119
61. LAUSANNE, SWITZERLAND 121
62. SIBIU, ROMANIA 124
63. LÜBECK, GERMANY 126
64. PALERMO, ITALY 128
65. YORK, ENGLAND 130
66. MONS, BELGIUM 132
67. DUNDEE, SCOTLAND 134
68. SOPOT, POLAND 136
69. BURSA, TURKEY 138
70. HUELVA, SPAIN 140
71. NIJMEGEN, NETHERLANDS 141
72. GUIMARAES, PORTUGAL 143
73. LARNACA, CYPRUS 145
74. DEBRECEN, HUNGARY 147
75. PESCARA, ITALY 149
76. YAROSLAVL, RUSSIA 151
77. HRADEC KRALOVE, CZECH REPUBLIC 153
78. FARO, PORTUGAL 155
79. NORWICH, ENGLAND 157
80. OHRID, NORTH MACEDONIA 159
81. WUPPERTAL, GERMANY 161
82. RUSE, BULGARIA 163

83.	ZADAR, CROATIA	165
84.	HUESCA, SPAIN	167
85.	FRIBOURG, SWITZERLAND	169
86.	DURHAM, ENGLAND	171
87.	RENNES, FRANCE	173
88.	OSTRAVA, CZECH REPUBLIC	175
89.	SOPRON, HUNGARY	176
90.	NIZHNY NOVGOROD, RUSSIA	178
91.	COMO, ITALY	180
92.	BANSKO, BULGARIA	182
93.	KAVALA, GREECE	184
94.	AARHUS, DENMARK	186
95.	PECS, HUNGARY	189
96.	COSENZA, ITALY	191
97.	LUGANO, SWITZERLAND	193
98.	ESKILSTUNA, SWEDEN	195
99.	SKOPJE, NORTH MACEDONIA	196
100.	PORTO SANTO, PORTUGAL	198
101.	ST. GALLEN, SWITZERLAND	200
102.	ÅLESUND, NORWAY	202
103.	MODENA, ITALY	204
104.	SOCHI, RUSSIA	206
105.	MONSCHAU, GERMANY	208
106.	LA ROCHELLE, FRANCE	210
107.	TRENTO, ITALY	212
108.	KLAIPEDA, LITHUANIA	214
109.	BYDGOSZCZ, POLAND	216
110.	ALGHERO, ITALY	218

111. TALLINN, ESTONIA 220
112. TRABZON, TURKEY 222
113. SARANDA, ALBANIA 224
114. MAASTRICHT, NETHERLANDS 226
115. MATERA, ITALY 228
116. PLZEN, CZECH REPUBLIC 230
117. BRIGHTON, ENGLAND 232
118. SIGHISOARA, ROMANIA 234
119. KOTOR, MONTENEGRO 236
120. AMIENS, FRANCE 238
121. KURESSAARE, ESTONIA 240
122. RAVENNA, ITALY 242
123. MONTPELLIER, FRANCE 243
124. SIBENIK, CROATIA 246
125. KALMAR, SWEDEN 247
126. SZEGED, HUNGARY 249
127. KRASNOYARSK, RUSSIA 251
128. CORK, IRELAND 253
129. RETHYMNO, GREECE 255
130. VIANDEN, LUXEMBOURG 256
131. JÖNKÖPING, SWEDEN 259
132. PIRAN, SLOVENIA 261
133. SOLOTHURN, SWITZERLAND 263
134. GDANSK, POLAND 265
135. VENTSPILS, LATVIA 266
136. ERFURT, GERMANY 268
137. AVEIRO, PORTUGAL 270
138. LECCE, ITALY 272

139. DELFT, NETHERLANDS 273
140. BLED, SLOVENIA 275
141. OBAN, SCOTLAND 277
142. LEÓN, SPAIN 279
143. CHANIA, GREECE 281
144. KARLOVY VARY, CZECH REPUBLIC 283
145. KILKENNY, IRELAND 284
146. FUNCHAL, PORTUGAL 287
147. VLADIVOSTOK, RUSSIA 289
148. ADANA, TURKEY 291
149. GRONAU, GERMANY 292
150. RIJEKA, CROATIA 294

GIRONA, SPAIN

Girona is a beautiful city located in northeastern Catalonia, Spain. With its rich history, stunning architecture, and vibrant culture, Girona is a perfect destination for travelers seeking an authentic Spanish experience. Here is everything you need to know about this enchanting city.

GETTING TO GIRONA

Girona is easily accessible by both air and train. The Girona-Costa Brava airport is only a short distance from the city center, and there are regular flights to major European cities. Alternatively, you can take a high-speed train from Barcelona or other major cities in Spain.

EXPLORING THE CITY

Girona's historic center is a maze of narrow streets, alleys, and plazas. The city's most famous landmark is its ancient walls, which date back to the Roman period. Walking along the walls provides stunning views of the city and the surrounding countryside. Other must-see attractions include the Gothic Cathedral of Santa Maria, the Arab Baths, and the Jewish Quarter.

FOOD AND DRINK

Girona is renowned for its traditional Catalan cuisine, which emphasizes fresh, locally sourced ingredients. The city is home to numerous restaurants and cafes serving everything from tapas to fine dining. Be sure to try some of the local specialties, such as botifarra, a type of sausage, and coca de vidre, a sweet pastry.

SHOPPING

Girona is a shopper's paradise, with a wide variety of shops selling everything from fashion to souvenirs. The city's old town is home to many boutique stores selling unique, handmade items. The city's markets are also worth a visit, offering fresh produce, handmade crafts, and local specialties.

EVENTS AND FESTIVALS

Girona hosts numerous events and festivals throughout the year, celebrating everything from music to food. The city's most famous festival is the Temps de Flors, or "Time of Flowers," which takes place in May. During this festival, the city's streets and public spaces are filled with colorful floral displays.

ACCOMMODATION

Girona offers a wide range of accommodation options, from budget-friendly hostels to luxurious hotels. Many of the city's hotels are located in historic buildings, providing a unique and authentic experience.

IN CONCLUSION

Girona is a charming city with a rich history and vibrant culture. Whether you're interested in exploring its ancient walls, trying its delicious cuisine, or simply soaking up the atmosphere, Girona has something for everyone. So why not add this gem of a city to your travel itinerary?

WROCLAW, POLAND

If you're planning a trip to Poland, don't miss out on Wroclaw, one of the country's most charming and vibrant cities. Located in western Poland, Wroclaw is known for its beautiful architecture, lively cultural scene, and friendly locals. Here are some reasons why Wroclaw should be on your travel itinerary.

HISTORY AND CULTURE

Wroclaw has a long and fascinating history that can be seen in its many historical landmarks and attractions. The city's most iconic symbol is the Market Square, a UNESCO World Heritage Site that dates back to the 13th century. It's home to colorful buildings, charming cafes, and a bustling market where you can find everything from handmade crafts to fresh produce.

The city also has an impressive collection of museums, including the National Museum, which houses a vast collection of Polish art, and the Panorama of the Battle of Racławice, a 19th-century painting that depicts a key battle in Poland's fight for independence.

FOOD AND DRINK

Polish cuisine is hearty and satisfying, and Wroclaw is no exception. The city is known for its pierogi, a traditional Polish dish made with dough and filled with meat, cheese, or vegetables. You can find pierogi at almost any restaurant in the city, but for the best experience, head to Pierogarnia Stary Młyn, a charming eatery that specializes in these delicious dumplings.

Wroclaw is also home to a thriving craft beer scene, with several microbreweries and pubs that serve up delicious local brews. Check out Browar Stu Mostów or Spiż for some of the city's best beer.

ENTERTAINMENT AND NIGHTLIFE

Wroclaw is a city that knows how to have fun. Its cultural scene is alive and well, with numerous theaters, cinemas, and music venues that offer a diverse range of performances. The city is also home to several annual festivals, including the Wroclaw Jazz Festival and the Brave Festival, which celebrates the music and culture of indigenous people from around the world.

At night, the city comes alive with its vibrant nightlife. From cozy pubs to chic cocktail bars, there's something for everyone. For a truly unique experience, check out Prohibicja, a speakeasy-style bar that requires a password to enter.

CONCLUSION

Wroclaw is a city that's full of surprises. Its rich history, delicious cuisine, and lively cultural scene make it a must-visit destination in Poland. Whether you're a history buff, a foodie, or just looking for a good time, Wroclaw has something for everyone. So pack your bags and get ready to discover the charm of this amazing city.

PORTO, PORTUGAL

Porto, also known as Oporto, is a beautiful and charming city located on the northwestern coast of Portugal. This vibrant city is known for its rich history, unique culture, and stunning architecture, making it a popular destination for tourists from all over the world. Whether you're looking to soak up the local culture, indulge in the delicious cuisine, or simply explore the beautiful scenery, Porto has something to offer for everyone.

GETTING TO PORTO

Porto is well-connected to major European cities and can be easily reached by air, train, or car. The city's Francisco Sá Carneiro Airport is located just 15 minutes from the city center and serves several major airlines. Alternatively, you can take a train from Lisbon or other parts of Portugal to reach Porto, which offers a scenic journey through the beautiful countryside.

CULTURE AND HISTORY

Porto has a rich history that dates back to the Roman times, and its historic center is a UNESCO World Heritage Site. The city's iconic landmarks include the stunning Clerigos Tower, the beautiful Lello Bookstore, and the historic Ribeira District, which is home to several picturesque cafes and restaurants. Porto is also known for its unique culture, which is evident in its traditional music, art, and cuisine.

DELICIOUS CUISINE

Porto is a food lover's paradise, offering a range of delicious local cuisine. The city is famous for its Port wine, which is produced in the Douro Valley and is best enjoyed with traditional dishes such as bacalhau (salt cod), francesinha (a sandwich with various meats and cheese), and cozido (a hearty stew). Porto is also home to several Michelin-starred restaurants, which offer a fine dining experience for those looking to indulge.

BEAUTIFUL SCENERY

Porto is surrounded by stunning natural scenery, including the Douro Valley, which is home to several vineyards and offers breathtaking views of the river and the valley. The city's beaches, such as Matosinhos and Foz do Douro, are perfect for sunbathing and swimming, while the city's parks and gardens, such as the Crystal Palace Gardens and the Serralves Park, offer a peaceful escape from the hustle and bustle of the city.

CONCLUSION

Porto is a beautiful and charming city that offers a unique blend of culture, history, cuisine, and scenery. Whether you're looking to explore the city's historic landmarks, indulge in the delicious cuisine, or simply soak up the beautiful scenery, Porto has something to offer for everyone. So, pack your bags and head to Porto for an unforgettable travel experience.

GHENT, BELGIUM

Ghent is a vibrant and historic city located in the Flemish region of Belgium. Known for its stunning medieval architecture, lively culture, and picturesque canals, Ghent is an excellent destination for travelers looking to explore Belgium beyond its capital city of Brussels. In this guide, we'll take a closer look at what makes Ghent such a unique and unforgettable place to visit.

EXPLORING GHENT'S OLD TOWN

Ghent's Old Town is the heart of the city, and it's where you'll find most of the city's historical landmarks, museums, and cultural attractions. The Gravensteen Castle is a must-see attraction that dates back to the 12th century, and it offers breathtaking views of the city. The St. Bavo's Cathedral is another landmark that's worth visiting, as it houses several famous works of art, including the world-renowned Ghent Altarpiece.

GHENT'S CANAL DISTRICT

Ghent's canal district is one of the city's most picturesque areas, and it's a great place to take a stroll or enjoy a boat tour. The canals are lined with beautiful buildings and quaint cafes, and they offer a unique perspective on the city's history and architecture.

THE BEST OF GHENT'S CUISINE

Belgium is known for its delicious cuisine, and Ghent is no exception. From traditional Belgian waffles to hearty Flemish stews, the city has a wide variety of dishes to try. One local specialty that you shouldn't miss is Ghent's famous "Tierenteyn" mustard, which has been produced in the city for over 200 years.

GHENT'S NIGHTLIFE

Ghent's nightlife is lively and diverse, with options ranging from cozy pubs to trendy bars and nightclubs. The city's student population ensures that there's always a vibrant atmosphere, and the variety of venues means that there's something for everyone.

GETTING AROUND GHENT

Ghent is a compact city, and most of its attractions can be reached on foot or by bike. The city also has an extensive public transportation system, including buses and trams, which makes it easy to explore the city and its surrounding areas.

FINAL THOUGHTS

Ghent is a hidden gem that offers travelers a unique blend of history, culture, and modernity. Whether you're interested in exploring the city's medieval architecture or enjoying its vibrant nightlife, Ghent has something for everyone. So why not add it to your travel itinerary and discover the best of this charming Belgian city?

TIMISOARA, ROMANIA

Timisoara is a city located in the western part of Romania and is known for its rich history, diverse culture, and impressive architecture. It is a hidden gem waiting to be discovered by travelers looking for something unique and off the beaten path. In this article, we will explore what makes Timisoara a must-visit destination.

HISTORY AND CULTURE

Timisoara is a city with a rich history dating back to the Roman Empire. It was later conquered by the Ottoman Empire, which left a significant impact on the city's architecture and culture. Timisoara was also the first city in Europe to have electric street lighting, earning it the nickname "The City of Light." Today, Timisoara is a multicultural city with a vibrant arts scene, hosting various cultural events and festivals throughout the year.

ARCHITECTURE

Timisoara's architecture is a mix of styles, including Baroque, Art Nouveau, and modernist. One of the city's most impressive buildings is the Timisoara Orthodox Cathedral, built in the Byzantine style with golden domes and intricate frescoes. The city's main square, Piata Unirii, is also worth a visit, with its colorful buildings and impressive fountains.

PARKS AND GARDENS

Timisoara is home to several beautiful parks and gardens, providing a peaceful escape from the hustle and bustle of the city. The Botanical Park is a must-visit, with its stunning collection of plants from all over the world. The Roses Park is another popular destination, with its beautiful rose gardens and tranquil atmosphere.

FOOD AND DRINK

Romanian cuisine is a fusion of various cultures, including Turkish, Hungarian, and Balkan. Timisoara is home to several restaurants and cafes serving traditional Romanian dishes, including sarmale (stuffed cabbage rolls) and mititei (grilled sausages). The city is also known for its local beers, with several microbreweries producing craft beers.

FINAL THOUGHTS

Timisoara is a hidden gem in Romania, offering travelers a unique and authentic experience. Whether you're interested in history, culture, architecture, nature, or food, Timisoara has something for everyone. So, the next time you're planning a trip to Europe, be sure to add Timisoara to your itinerary.

TRIESTE, ITALY

Trieste, an enchanting city located in the northeastern part of Italy, is a perfect destination for travelers seeking a mix of history, culture, and natural beauty. Known for its rich past and multicultural heritage, the city has become a popular tourist destination in recent years. In this article, we will guide you through the must-visit places and activities that will make your trip to Trieste unforgettable.

HISTORY

Trieste's history dates back to the Roman Empire, and the city has been ruled by various empires throughout the centuries. As a result, Trieste has a unique blend of architectural styles and cultural influences. A visit to the city's historic center will take you back in time as you stroll through the narrow alleys and squares adorned with beautiful Baroque and Neoclassical buildings. The Piazza Unità d'Italia, the largest seaside square in Europe, is a must-see landmark that offers a panoramic view of the Adriatic Sea.

CULTURE

Trieste's multicultural heritage is evident in its diverse cuisine, traditions, and festivals. The city is home to numerous museums, galleries, and theaters that showcase its rich artistic and literary heritage. The Teatro Romano, a well-preserved Roman theater, and the Museo Revoltella, a contemporary art museum, are popular cultural attractions. The city's annual Barcolana regatta, which attracts thousands of visitors, is a colorful festival that celebrates Trieste's maritime history.

NATURAL BEAUTY

Surrounded by the stunning landscapes of the Carso plateau and the Adriatic Sea, Trieste offers plenty of opportunities for outdoor activities. The Miramare Castle, a 19th-century palace, is situated on a cliff overlooking the sea and offers breathtaking views of the Gulf of Trieste. The Grotta Gigante, one of the largest caves in the world, is a natural wonder that is a short drive from the city. The Rilke Trail, a scenic walking path along the cliffs, offers a peaceful retreat from the bustling city.

CUISINE

Trieste's cuisine is a blend of Italian, Austrian, and Slovenian influences, resulting in a unique gastronomic experience. The city is renowned for its coffee culture and seafood dishes, such as sarde in saor and baccalà alla triestina. The traditional drink of Trieste is the aperitif known as Spritz, a refreshing cocktail made with Prosecco, Aperol, and soda water.

CONCLUSION

Trieste is a charming city that offers a diverse range of experiences to its visitors. From its rich history and culture to its stunning natural beauty and delicious cuisine, Trieste has something for everyone. We hope this guide will inspire you to explore this hidden gem of Italy and make unforgettable memories.

RIGA, LATVIA

Riga is the capital and largest city of Latvia, situated on the coast of the Baltic Sea in Northern Europe. It is a city with a rich history, beautiful architecture, and a vibrant cultural scene that makes it a must-visit destination for travelers.

HISTORICAL SIGNIFICANCE OF RIGA

The city of Riga was founded in the 13th century by German crusaders, who established a fortress on the banks of the Daugava River. Riga quickly grew into a prosperous trading center, attracting merchants from all over Europe. Over the centuries, Riga has been ruled by various powers including Swedes, Poles, and Russians, each of whom left their mark on the city's architecture and culture.

ATTRACTIONS AND ACTIVITIES

One of the main attractions of Riga is its Old Town, which is a UNESCO World Heritage site. The old town is full of narrow streets, beautiful buildings, and stunning churches, making it a perfect place to wander around and get lost in the city's history. Some of the must-visit landmarks in Riga include the Riga Castle, the St. Peter's

Church, the House of the Blackheads, and the Latvian National Opera.

Riga is also known for its Art Nouveau architecture, with over a third of the buildings in the city center designed in this style. The Alberta iela street is especially famous for its Art Nouveau buildings and is a popular spot for taking photographs.

Apart from sightseeing, Riga has a lot to offer in terms of food, nightlife, and culture. The Central Market is a great place to try Latvian cuisine and sample local delicacies, while the city's many bars and clubs make it a fun place to party. Riga also hosts several cultural events throughout the year, such as the Latvian Song and Dance Festival, which showcases traditional Latvian music and dance.

GETTING AROUND

Riga is a compact city, and most of the main attractions are within walking distance of each other. However, the city also has an efficient public transportation system, including buses, trams, and trolleybuses, which are all easily accessible and affordable.

CONCLUSION

In conclusion, Riga is a city full of history, culture, and beauty, making it a perfect destination for travelers. Whether you're interested in architecture, food, nightlife, or just exploring a new city, Riga has something for everyone. So, pack your bags and get ready to discover the enchanting city of Riga!

LILLE, FRANCE

Lille is a charming city located in the northern region of France. It is a vibrant and bustling city that is well-known for its historical landmarks, excellent shopping and dining options, and warm and welcoming locals. Whether you are a history buff or just looking for a memorable vacation destination, Lille is a must-visit city.

GETTING THERE

Lille is easily accessible from major cities in Europe, with direct train connections to London, Paris, Brussels, and Amsterdam. If you are arriving by air, the Lille-Lesquin Airport is conveniently located just outside the city and is served by several airlines.

EXPLORING LILLE

The city is known for its grand architecture, lively squares, and bustling streets. The historic center of Lille, known as Vieux-Lille, is a must-visit area. Here, you can stroll through the narrow, winding streets and admire the beautiful 17th-century Flemish-style buildings. The Place du Général de Gaulle, also known as the Grand Place, is a bustling square surrounded by stunning buildings and is a perfect spot for people-watching.

The Musée des Beaux-Arts de Lille is a must-visit for art lovers. The museum houses a vast collection of artwork from the 15th century to the present day, including paintings by Rubens, Delacroix, and Van Gogh. Another must-visit landmark is the Citadel of Lille, a massive fortification built in the 17th century.

SHOPPING AND DINING

Lille is a shopper's paradise, with an abundance of shopping options ranging from high-end boutiques to charming local markets. The Rue de la Grande Chaussée and the Rue de Bethune are popular shopping streets, while the Marché de Wazemmes is a lively market where you can find everything from fresh produce to vintage clothing.

The city is also a foodie's delight, with an array of dining options ranging from traditional French cuisine to international flavors. The city is famous for its waffles, which can be found at many cafes and street stalls throughout the city.

CONCLUSION

Lille is a city full of charm, history, and culture. From its beautiful architecture and museums to its excellent shopping and dining options, there is something for everyone to enjoy. Plan your trip today and discover the magic of Lille.

GOTHENBURG, SWEDEN

Gothenburg, situated on the west coast of Sweden, is a bustling city that offers a mix of traditional and modern culture. It is the second-largest city in Sweden and boasts a lively arts scene, a thriving food culture, and an array of stunning outdoor spaces. Here are some of the top things to see and do in Gothenburg:

GETTING AROUND

Getting around Gothenburg is easy thanks to its efficient public transportation system. The city's extensive network of trams, buses, and boats makes it easy to get to all the major attractions.

EXPLORE HAGA

One of the oldest neighborhoods in Gothenburg, Haga is a picturesque district with cobbled streets and colorful wooden houses. It's the perfect place to spend a few hours browsing the boutiques, cafes, and antique shops.

VISIT LISEBERG

Liseberg is one of the largest amusement parks in Scandinavia and is home to over 40 rides and attractions, including roller coasters, carousels, and arcade games. It's a fun day out for all the family.

DISCOVER THE ART SCENE

Gothenburg has a thriving art scene, with numerous galleries and museums showcasing contemporary and traditional art. The Gothenburg Museum of Art is a must-visit for any art lover, with an impressive collection of Nordic and international works.

GO ISLAND HOPPING

Gothenburg's archipelago is made up of over 20 islands, each with its own unique charm. Take a boat trip to explore the islands and discover hidden beaches, fishing villages, and scenic hikes.

INDULGE IN THE FOOD CULTURE

Gothenburg's food scene is known for its fresh seafood, artisanal coffee, and craft beer. The city is home to several Michelin-starred restaurants, as well as more casual eateries serving up traditional Swedish cuisine.

CONCLUSION

Gothenburg is a vibrant and exciting city that offers something for everyone. Whether you're interested in art, food, or outdoor adventures, you're sure to find plenty to keep you entertained. With its efficient public transportation, friendly locals, and stunning scenery, Gothenburg is the perfect destination for your next vacation.

NANTES, FRANCE

Nantes is a beautiful city located in western France, on the banks of the Loire River. With its rich history, vibrant culture, and stunning architecture, Nantes has become a popular tourist destination for travelers from all over the world. If you're planning a trip to France, here are some things you shouldn't miss when visiting Nantes.

GETTING TO NANTES

The easiest way to get to Nantes is by flying into Nantes Atlantique Airport. Alternatively, you can take a train from Paris, which takes about two and a half hours. Once you arrive, the city is easily navigable by foot, bike, or public transportation.

EXPLORING THE CITY

There is plenty to see and do in Nantes, whether you're interested in history, art, or just soaking up the local atmosphere. One of the city's most famous landmarks is the Chateau des Ducs de Bretagne, a magnificent castle that dates back to the 15th century. The castle now houses a museum that explores the history of Nantes and the surrounding region.

Another must-see attraction is the Les Machines de l'Île, a unique park that combines art and technology to create giant mechanical animals and other incredible structures. Visitors can take a ride on the back of a mechanical elephant or explore the intricate workings of a giant spider.

For a taste of local culture, head to the Passage Pommeraye, a stunning 19th-century shopping arcade that is home to a variety of boutiques and cafes. You can also visit the Marche de Talensac, a bustling market that sells everything from fresh produce to handmade crafts.

FOOD AND DRINK

No trip to France would be complete without sampling the local cuisine, and Nantes has plenty to offer in terms of food and drink. Be sure to try the local specialty, galette saucisse, a savory crepe filled with sausage and served with mustard. You can also sample the region's famous Muscadet wine, which pairs perfectly with seafood.

CONCLUSION

Whether you're interested in history, art, or simply enjoying the local culture, Nantes has something for everyone. With its stunning architecture, unique attractions, and delicious cuisine, this charming city is a must-visit destination for any traveler exploring the beauty of France.

PLOVDIV, BULGARIA

Plovdiv, located in southern Bulgaria, is one of the oldest continuously inhabited cities in Europe. Its history spans over 8,000 years, with evidence of Neolithic settlements and a thriving Roman era. Today, Plovdiv is a vibrant cultural and economic center, attracting tourists from all over the world.

GETTING THERE AND AROUND

Plovdiv is accessible by bus, train, and car from major Bulgarian cities such as Sofia and Burgas. The city has a well-developed public transportation system, including trams, buses, and trolleybuses, making it easy to explore the city's sights.

SIGHTS AND ATTRACTIONS

Plovdiv's Old Town is a maze of cobbled streets, colorful houses, and ancient ruins. The city's most famous landmark is the Roman Amphitheater, which is still used for concerts and cultural events. Another must-see is the Ancient Stadium, which hosted games during the Roman era. The Old Town also features numerous museums, art galleries, and souvenir shops.

FOOD AND DRINK

Bulgarian cuisine is a delicious blend of Mediterranean and Balkan flavors. In Plovdiv, visitors can indulge in traditional dishes such as banitsa, a savory pastry filled with cheese or spinach, and kavarma, a hearty stew made with meat and vegetables. For dessert, try baklava, a sweet pastry made with layers of phyllo dough and honey. Plovdiv also boasts a vibrant nightlife scene, with plenty of bars and clubs to choose from.

ACCOMMODATIONS

Plovdiv offers a range of accommodations, from budget-friendly hostels to luxury hotels. The Old Town has numerous guesthouses and boutique hotels, many of which are housed in historic buildings. For those seeking modern amenities, there are plenty of hotels and apartments in the city center.

CONCLUSION

Plovdiv is a fascinating destination for travelers looking to explore Bulgaria's rich history and culture. With its ancient ruins, charming Old Town, and delicious cuisine, there's something for everyone in this vibrant city.

VALENCIA, SPAIN

Valencia City is a beautiful and historic city located in eastern Spain. It is the third-largest city in Spain and is known for its stunning architecture, delicious food, and lively atmosphere. If you are planning a trip to Spain, here are some reasons why you should consider visiting Valencia City.

THE CITY'S VIBRANT CULTURE

Valencia City has a rich cultural heritage that is reflected in its art, architecture, and traditions. The city is famous for its unique festivals, such as Las Fallas, where giant paper-mache figures are paraded around the city before being burned in a spectacular fireworks display. Visitors can also enjoy the City of Arts and Sciences, a modern complex of futuristic buildings that house an opera house, an IMAX cinema, and a science museum.

THE CULINARY SCENE

Valencia City is known for its delicious food, and it is the birthplace of the famous Spanish dish paella. Paella is a rice dish that is cooked with saffron, chicken, rabbit, and vegetables. Visitors can sample this dish at one of the many restaurants in the city, or they can visit the Central Market, where they can buy fresh ingredients to make their own paella.

HISTORICAL LANDMARKS

Valencia City has a rich history, and there are many historical landmarks that visitors can explore. The most famous landmark is the City of Arts and Sciences, but there are also many other notable buildings, such as the Cathedral of Valencia and the Torres de Quart. Visitors can also take a stroll through the charming old town, which is filled with narrow streets, colorful buildings, and quaint shops.

THE BEACHES

Valencia City is located on the Mediterranean coast, and it is home to some beautiful beaches. The most popular beach is Malvarrosa, which is a long, wide beach with golden sand and clear blue water. Visitors can relax on the beach, swim in the sea, or take a stroll along the promenade.

CONCLUSION

Valencia City is a must-visit destination in Spain. Its vibrant culture, delicious food, historical landmarks, and beautiful beaches make it an ideal place to explore. Whether you are interested in art and architecture, history and tradition, or simply relaxing on the beach, Valencia City has something for everyone.

UTRECHT, NETHERLANDS

Utrecht is a charming city in the Netherlands that offers a perfect blend of history, culture, and modernity. Situated in the heart of the country, Utrecht is a popular destination for tourists who want to experience the Dutch way of life. With its picturesque canals, towering cathedrals, and vibrant cafes, the city has something to offer everyone.

RICH HISTORY

Utrecht has a rich history that dates back to the Roman era. As such, the city boasts a variety of historical sites, including the Dom Tower, which is the tallest church tower in the Netherlands. The Dom Tower was built in the 14th century and offers a panoramic view of the city. The city also has a number of museums that showcase its rich history, including the Museum Catharijneconvent, which houses an impressive collection of religious art and artifacts.

VIBRANT CULTURE

Utrecht is a city that's rich in culture, and visitors can explore its vibrant arts scene by visiting one of its many galleries, theaters, and cultural events. The city has a thriving music scene, and visitors can enjoy live performances by local musicians in venues such as the TivoliVredenburg, which is one of the largest music venues in the country. Additionally, Utrecht is home to a variety of festivals throughout the year, including the International

Film Festival, the Holland Festival, and the Utrecht Early Music Festival.

MODERN AMENITIES

While Utrecht is steeped in history and culture, it's also a modern city that offers plenty of amenities for visitors. The city has a variety of shopping districts, including the Hoog Catharijne, which is the largest indoor shopping center in the country. Additionally, Utrecht has a diverse food scene, with a variety of restaurants serving cuisine from around the world. Visitors can also enjoy the city's many parks and outdoor spaces, including the beautiful Wilhelminapark.

GETTING AROUND

Utrecht is a compact city that's easy to explore on foot or by bike. Visitors can rent a bike from one of the many rental shops in the city and explore its many bike paths and trails. Alternatively, visitors can take advantage of the city's public transportation system, which includes buses and trams that run throughout the city.

CONCLUSION

In conclusion, Utrecht is a city that offers a perfect blend of history, culture, and modernity. With its rich history, vibrant culture, and modern amenities, Utrecht is a must-visit destination for anyone traveling to the Netherlands. Whether you're interested in exploring the city's historical sites, experiencing its vibrant arts scene, or simply enjoying its modern amenities, Utrecht has something to offer everyone.

SARAJEVO, BOSNIA AND HERZEGOVINA

Sarajevo, the capital of Bosnia and Herzegovina, is a city with a rich cultural and historical heritage. Known as the "Jerusalem of Europe" due to its diverse religious communities, Sarajevo is a fascinating destination for travelers seeking to immerse themselves in the unique cultural tapestry of the Balkans.

DISCOVERING THE OLD TOWN

One of the must-see attractions in Sarajevo is the Old Town, also known as Baščaršija. Here, visitors can wander through a maze of narrow streets and alleys lined with shops and cafes. Highlights of the Old Town include the Sebilj fountain, the Gazi Husrev-beg Mosque, and the historic Morića Han inn.

VISITING THE MUSEUMS

Sarajevo has a rich history, and visitors can learn more about it by visiting one of the city's many museums. The Museum of Sarajevo is a great place to start, offering exhibits on the city's history from prehistoric times to the present day. The Historical Museum of Bosnia and

Herzegovina is also worth a visit, showcasing the region's history from the medieval period to the present day.

EXPLORING THE FOOD SCENE

Sarajevo is known for its delicious food, which reflects the city's multicultural heritage. Local specialties include cevapi, a type of grilled sausage served with bread and onions, and burek, a savory pastry filled with meat, cheese, or spinach. Visitors can sample these dishes at local restaurants and cafes throughout the city.

EXPERIENCING THE NIGHTLIFE

Sarajevo has a vibrant nightlife scene, with bars and clubs catering to a range of tastes. Visitors can enjoy live music and cocktails at the Kriterion Cinema and Cafe, or dance the night away at Club Sloga, one of the city's most popular nightclubs.

CONCLUSION

Sarajevo is a city that offers something for everyone, from history buffs and foodies to nightlife enthusiasts. With its rich cultural heritage and friendly locals, it's a destination that is not to be missed.

KRAKOW, POLAND

Krakow is a fascinating city located in southern Poland that offers visitors a blend of historical architecture, cultural attractions, and natural beauty. Founded in the 7th century, Krakow has been one of Poland's most significant cultural and intellectual centers, with a rich heritage of art, literature, and music.

EXPLORING THE CITY'S OLD TOWN

Krakow's Old Town is a UNESCO World Heritage Site and is known for its cobblestone streets, charming cafes, and lively street performers. Visitors can explore the city's numerous museums and galleries, including the National Museum, the Wawel Royal Castle, and the Jewish Quarter's Galicia Jewish Museum.

A HUB FOR EUROPEAN HISTORY

Krakow has played a central role in European history, and visitors can explore some of its most significant landmarks and monuments. The city's most famous landmark is the Wawel Royal Castle, a stunning Renaissance-era palace that has been the seat of Polish kings for centuries. Other must-see historical sites include the Auschwitz-Birkenau Memorial and Museum and the Schindler's Factory Museum, both of which offer powerful insights into the region's past.

NATURAL SCENERIES

Krakow also boasts a wealth of natural beauty, including nearby mountain ranges, lakes, and forests. Visitors can explore the Tatra Mountains, hike along the stunning Pieniny National Park, or take a stroll along the picturesque Vistula River.

A CULINARY EXPERIENCE

Krakow is also known for its delicious cuisine, featuring hearty meat dishes, fresh seafood, and delectable pastries. Visitors can sample traditional Polish dishes, such as pierogi dumplings, bigos stew, and kielbasa sausage, at the city's many restaurants and cafes.

FINAL WORDS

Krakow is a charming and vibrant city that offers something for every type of traveler. Whether you're interested in exploring history, culture, or nature, you're sure to find something to love in this beautiful Polish city.

VILNIUS, LITHUANIA

Vilnius, the capital of Lithuania, is a fascinating destination that offers a rich blend of history, culture, and modernity. The city's historic Old Town, with its narrow cobbled streets and Baroque architecture, has been designated a UNESCO World Heritage Site, and it's not hard to see why. From its lively markets to its beautiful parks, Vilnius has something to offer every traveler.

HISTORY AND ARCHITECTURE

Vilnius is steeped in history, and the city's architecture reflects its varied past. Gothic, Renaissance, Baroque, and Neoclassical buildings line the streets, each with a unique story to tell. The city's most iconic landmarks include the Gediminas Castle Tower, the Church of St. Anne, and the Vilnius Cathedral. The Old Town is also home to numerous museums, including the National Museum of Lithuania and the Museum of Genocide Victims, which chronicles the city's Soviet past.

CULTURE AND ENTERTAINMENT

Vilnius is a city that knows how to have fun. The Lithuanian capital is home to a thriving arts scene, with numerous theaters, galleries, and music venues. Visitors can enjoy a night of jazz at the Vokieciu Street Jazz Club or catch a play at the Lithuanian National Drama Theater. The city also hosts a number of festivals throughout the year, including the Vilnius Jazz Festival and the Vilnius Street Musician's Day.

FOOD AND DRINK

Lithuanian cuisine is a fusion of Eastern European and Scandinavian flavors, and Vilnius offers visitors a wide range of culinary delights. Traditional dishes include cepelinai (potato dumplings filled with meat), kugelis (potato pudding), and saltibarsciai (cold beet soup). For those with a sweet tooth, the city's bakeries offer a variety of delicious pastries, including sakotis (a spiral-shaped cake) and šimtalapis (a layered cake). And no visit to Vilnius would be complete without trying a glass of local beer or a shot of honey liqueur.

NATURE AND PARKS

Despite its status as a capital city, Vilnius is surrounded by greenery. The city is home to numerous parks and gardens, including Vingis Park and Bernardine Gardens. Visitors can take a stroll along the banks of the River Neris or explore the nearby forests and lakes. The Verkiai Regional Park, located just outside the city, offers stunning views of the surrounding countryside and is a popular destination for hikers and nature lovers.

CONCLUSION

Vilnius is a city that has it all - history, culture, entertainment, food, and nature. Whether you're interested in exploring the city's rich past or sampling its delicious cuisine, there's something for everyone in this vibrant and welcoming city. So why not book your trip to Vilnius today and experience all that this fascinating destination has to offer?

BOLOGNA, ITALY

Bologna is a city in northern Italy known for its vibrant culture, stunning architecture, and delicious cuisine. It's the capital of the Emilia-Romagna region and home to a thriving university, making it a popular destination for tourists and students alike. Here's why you should consider adding Bologna to your travel itinerary.

THE ARCHITECTURE

Bologna's architecture is a testament to its rich history. The city's center is home to numerous medieval and Renaissance-era buildings, including the iconic Two Towers. These towers were constructed in the 12th century and are now a symbol of the city. The Piazza Maggiore is another must-see attraction, with its stunning Basilica di San Petronio and the Palazzo Comunale, which houses the city hall.

THE CUISINE

Bologna is often referred to as the "food capital" of Italy, and for good reason. The city is home to a variety of delicious dishes, including its famous Bolognese sauce, made with beef, pork, and tomatoes. Other must-try dishes include tortellini, mortadella, and tagliatelle al ragù. Make sure to pair your meal with a glass of Lambrusco, a sparkling red wine that's popular in the region.

THE CULTURE

Bologna is a vibrant city with a rich cultural scene. The city is home to numerous theaters, museums, and art galleries, including the Museo Civico Archeologico, which houses artifacts from the Etruscan, Roman, and Greek civilizations. The city is also known for its music scene, with numerous festivals and concerts taking place throughout the year.

THE UNIVERSITY

Bologna is home to the oldest university in Europe, the University of Bologna, which was founded in 1088. The university is still in operation today and attracts students from all over the world. Its stunning historic buildings, including the Archiginnasio, which houses the Anatomical Theater, make it a popular destination for tourists as well.

CONCLUSION

Bologna is a city that shouldn't be missed on any trip to Italy. With its stunning architecture, delicious cuisine, rich cultural scene, and historic university, there's something for everyone in this vibrant city. Whether you're a student or a tourist, Bologna is sure to leave a lasting impression on you.

TOULOUSE, FRANCE

Are you looking for a charming destination to visit in France? Look no further than Toulouse! Located in the southwestern part of France, Toulouse is a city with a rich history, a vibrant culture, and a lively atmosphere. Let's delve deeper into what makes Toulouse so special.

CULTURE AND HISTORY

Toulouse is a city with a fascinating history that dates back to the Roman era. Its rich culture is evident in its numerous museums, art galleries, and historical landmarks. Visit the famous Musée des Augustins, a former monastery that houses a vast collection of European art from the Middle Ages to the 20th century. Marvel at the stunning Basilique Saint-Sernin, a UNESCO World Heritage Site and the largest Romanesque church in Europe. Don't forget to explore the charming old town, known as the "Pink City" due to the color of the bricks used in many of its buildings.

FOOD AND DRINK

Toulouse is known for its delicious cuisine, especially its local specialty, cassoulet. This hearty stew is made with white beans, sausage, and duck or pork, and it's a must-try when visiting Toulouse. Don't forget to wash it down with a glass of red wine from the nearby vineyards of Gaillac or Fronton.

ENTERTAINMENT AND NIGHTLIFE

Toulouse is a city that knows how to have fun! Whether you're looking for a night out on the town or a more low-key evening, Toulouse has plenty of options. Visit the trendy Place Saint-Pierre for a drink and live music, or check out one of the city's many theaters for a show. If you're feeling lucky, head to the Casino Barrière Toulouse for some gambling fun.

NATURE AND OUTDOORS

Toulouse is surrounded by stunning natural beauty, making it an ideal destination for outdoor enthusiasts. Take a stroll along the Canal du Midi, a UNESCO World Heritage Site that stretches for over 240 kilometers. Visit the Jardin des Plantes, a beautiful botanical garden in the heart of the city. And if you're up for a bit of a hike, head to the nearby Pyrenees Mountains for some breathtaking views.

CONCLUSION

Toulouse is a city that truly has something for everyone. With its rich history, delicious food and drink, lively entertainment, and beautiful natural surroundings, it's a destination that's not to be missed. Book your trip today and experience the enchanting Toulouse for yourself!

CLUJ-NAPOCA, ROMANIA

Cluj-Napoca is one of Romania's largest and most vibrant cities, situated in the northwestern part of the country. Known for its rich history, stunning architecture, and vibrant cultural scene, Cluj-Napoca is a must-visit destination for anyone interested in exploring the beauty and charm of Eastern Europe.

HISTORY AND CULTURE

Founded over 2,000 years ago, Cluj-Napoca is steeped in history and culture. The city has been ruled by various civilizations, including the Romans, the Hungarians, and the Austro-Hungarian Empire. Today, Cluj-Napoca boasts an impressive array of museums, galleries, and historical landmarks, including the National Museum of Transylvanian History, the Ethnographic Museum of Transylvania, and the Saint Michael's Church, one of the most beautiful Gothic churches in Romania.

FOOD AND DRINK

Cluj-Napoca is also a culinary destination, with an impressive selection of restaurants, cafes, and bars. Local specialties include paprika-spiced sausage, stuffed cabbage rolls, and traditional goulash. The city is also home to a thriving craft beer scene, with several microbreweries producing unique and flavorful beers.

NATURE AND SCENERY

Despite being a bustling city, Cluj-Napoca is surrounded by beautiful natural landscapes, including the Apuseni Mountains, the Turda Gorges, and the Salina Turda salt mine. The city also has several parks and green spaces, such as the Central Park and the Botanical Garden, where visitors can relax and enjoy nature.

EVENTS AND FESTIVALS

Cluj-Napoca is known for its lively cultural scene and hosts several annual events and festivals, such as the Transylvania International Film Festival, the Electric Castle music festival, and the Untold music festival, which attracts thousands of visitors from around the world.

IN CONCLUSION

Cluj-Napoca is a fascinating and diverse city with something to offer for everyone. Whether you're interested in history, culture, nature, or simply want to experience the vibrant atmosphere of Eastern Europe, Cluj-Napoca is a destination worth exploring.

INNSBRUCK, AUSTRIA

Nestled in the heart of the Austrian Alps, Innsbruck city is a beautiful and vibrant destination that is perfect for travelers seeking a mix of culture, history, and adventure. With its stunning mountain scenery, fascinating historical sites, and lively cultural scene, Innsbruck has something for everyone.

GETTING TO INNSBRUCK

Innsbruck is conveniently located in the western part of Austria and is easily accessible by plane, train, or car. The city has its own airport, Innsbruck Airport, which is served by a number of airlines. Visitors can also reach Innsbruck by train from major cities in Austria, as well as from neighboring countries such as Germany, Italy, and Switzerland.

EXPLORING THE OLD TOWN

One of the highlights of any visit to Innsbruck is exploring the Old Town, which is a charming and picturesque area that is steeped in history. The Old Town is home to a number of historic buildings and monuments, including the Golden Roof, which is one of the city's most iconic landmarks. Visitors can also explore the Imperial Palace, which was once the residence of the Habsburg monarchs, as well as the Hofburg, which is a grand imperial palace that now houses several museums.

EXPERIENCING THE ALPINE SCENERY

Innsbruck is surrounded by stunning mountain scenery, and visitors can take advantage of this by exploring the nearby Alps. There are a number of hiking trails and cable cars that offer breathtaking views of the mountains, and visitors can also enjoy skiing and snowboarding in the winter months. The Nordkette cable car, which departs from the city center, takes visitors up to the top of the nearby mountain, where they can enjoy panoramic views of the city and the surrounding mountains.

SAMPLING LOCAL CUISINE

Innsbruck is known for its delicious cuisine, and visitors should definitely take the time to sample some of the local specialties. One of the most popular dishes is Tiroler Gröstl, which is a hearty meal made with potatoes, beef, and onions. Visitors can also enjoy traditional Austrian dishes such as Wiener Schnitzel and Kaiserschmarrn, which is a sweet dish made with shredded pancakes and served with fruit compote.

CONCLUSION

Innsbruck city is a destination that offers something for everyone, from history and culture to adventure and cuisine. With its stunning mountain scenery, fascinating historical sites, and delicious cuisine, it's no wonder that Innsbruck is such a popular destination for travelers. So why not plan your visit to this beautiful Alpine jewel and discover all that it has to offer?

BRUGES, BELGIUM

Bruges, also known as the "Venice of the North," is a charming city located in the northwest of Belgium. The city is famous for its picturesque canals, cobbled streets, medieval architecture, and rich history. Bruges is one of the most popular tourist destinations in Europe and attracts millions of visitors every year.

GETTING THERE AND GETTING AROUND

Bruges is easily accessible by train or car from Brussels, Antwerp, or Ghent. The city is also well connected to major airports, including Brussels Airport and Ostend-Bruges International Airport. Once you're in Bruges, the best way to explore the city is on foot or by bike. You can also take a boat tour to see the city from a different perspective.

HISTORY AND ARCHITECTURE

Bruges is a city steeped in history, and its medieval architecture is well-preserved. The historic center of Bruges has been designated a UNESCO World Heritage Site. Some of the must-visit historical landmarks in the city include the Belfry Tower, the Church of Our Lady, and the Basilica of the Holy Blood.

CULINARY DELIGHTS

Belgium is known for its beer, chocolate, and waffles, and Bruges offers a plethora of culinary delights to satisfy your taste buds. Make sure to try the local brews, such as the Brugse Zot, and sample some of the city's famous chocolate at one of the many chocolate shops. You can also indulge in some freshly-made Belgian waffles topped with whipped cream and strawberries.

PARKS AND GARDENS

Bruges is home to several parks and gardens, which provide a tranquil escape from the city's bustling streets. The Minnewater Park, located in the heart of the city, is a popular spot for picnics and strolls. The Koningin Astridpark and the Sint-Annarei Park are also worth a visit.

BOUTIQUE STORES

Bruges is home to many boutique stores selling unique items such as handmade chocolates, lace, and ceramics. You can find these stores in the city's historic center, especially around the Markt and the Burg.

IN CONCLUSION

Bruges is a city that will enchant you with its beautiful canals, stunning architecture, and rich history. Whether you're interested in history, food, or just want to relax in a beautiful setting, Bruges has something to offer everyone. So, pack your bags, and don't miss out on the opportunity to explore this enchanting city.

HELSINKI, FINLAND

Helsinki, the capital of Finland, is a fascinating blend of modernity and tradition. Located on the shores of the Gulf of Finland, Helsinki is a vibrant city with a rich history, stunning architecture, and a lively cultural scene. From its beautiful parks and museums to its cutting-edge design and fashion, Helsinki has something for everyone. Here's a guide to exploring this Nordic gem.

GETTING AROUND

Getting around Helsinki is easy thanks to its excellent public transportation system, which includes buses, trams, and a metro. The Helsinki Card is an excellent way to save money and time, offering unlimited transportation and free admission to many museums and attractions. For an eco-friendlier way to explore the city, consider renting a bicycle or hopping on an electric scooter.

ATTRACTIONS AND SIGHTS

Helsinki is home to some of the most iconic landmarks in Finland, including the Helsinki Cathedral, the Sibelius Monument, and the Temppeliaukio Church. Architecture enthusiasts will love exploring the city's Art Nouveau and neoclassical buildings, while nature lovers can relax in the city's many parks and green spaces, such as Esplanadi Park and Kaivopuisto Park.

CULTURE AND ARTS

Helsinki is a cultural hub, with a vibrant arts and music scene. The city has many museums, including the Ateneum Art Museum, the Museum of Contemporary Art Kiasma, and the National Museum of Finland. Music lovers will appreciate the Finnish National Opera and the Helsinki Philharmonic Orchestra, while theater enthusiasts will enjoy the many productions at the Helsinki City Theatre.

FOOD AND DRINK

Finnish cuisine is a unique blend of Scandinavian, Russian, and European influences. Helsinki's restaurants offer a range of traditional and modern dishes, with a focus on fresh, locally sourced ingredients. Be sure to try Finnish specialties like reindeer meat and smoked salmon, and don't forget to sample some of the city's famous coffee and pastries.

SHOPPING

Helsinki is a shopper's paradise, with everything from luxury boutiques to quirky design shops. The Design District is a must-visit for anyone interested in Scandinavian design, while the Market Square is a great place to pick up fresh produce and souvenirs. The Kamppi shopping center and the Stockmann department store are also popular destinations for retail therapy.

CONCLUSION

Helsinki is a charming and dynamic city that offers visitors a unique blend of history, culture, and modernity. Whether you're interested in architecture, food, shopping, or the arts, Helsinki has something for everyone. So pack your bags and head to Finland's capital city - you won't be disappointed!

TARTU, ESTONIA

Tartu is a beautiful and historic city located in southern Estonia. It is the second-largest city in the country and is renowned for its rich cultural heritage, stunning architecture, and vibrant university life. Tartu is a popular destination for travelers who seek to explore the fascinating history, culture, and natural beauty of Estonia.

HISTORY AND CULTURE

Tartu is a city with a long and colorful history, which can be traced back to the 13th century. It has been an important cultural, educational, and commercial center throughout the centuries. Today, Tartu is known for its excellent museums, art galleries, theaters, and music festivals. The city is home to the University of Tartu, one of the oldest and most prestigious universities in the Baltic

States, which attracts many students and scholars from all over the world.

SIGHTS AND ATTRACTIONS

There are many things to see and do in Tartu, including visiting its historical sites, museums, and parks. The Old Town of Tartu is a charming and picturesque area with cobbled streets, colorful houses, and beautiful churches. The Tartu Art Museum, the Estonian National Museum, and the Tartu City Museum are must-visit destinations for history and art lovers.

The University of Tartu Botanical Gardens is another popular attraction, which features a vast collection of plants and flowers from all over the world. Other notable sights include the Toomemägi Park, the Angel's Bridge, and the Tartu Cathedral.

FOOD AND DRINK

Tartu is also a great destination for foodies, offering a wide range of local and international cuisines. The city has many excellent restaurants, cafes, and bars that serve traditional Estonian dishes as well as international cuisine. Some popular local dishes include black pudding, potato salad, and rye bread.

NIGHTLIFE

Tartu is famous for its vibrant nightlife, with many bars, pubs, and clubs catering to all tastes and preferences. The city has a lively music scene, with many local bands and musicians performing regularly in various venues around the city. The nightlife in Tartu is particularly popular among university students, who enjoy the lively atmosphere and affordable prices.

CONCLUSION

Tartu is a fascinating city with a rich history, beautiful architecture, and vibrant cultural scene. Whether you're interested in history, culture, or simply want to experience the charm and hospitality of Estonia, Tartu is an excellent destination to explore. From its historical sites and museums to its vibrant nightlife and culinary scene, there's something for everyone in Tartu.

LJUBLJANA, SLOVENIA

Nestled in the heart of Europe, Ljubljana, the capital city of Slovenia, is a vibrant and charming destination waiting to be explored. This picturesque city is known for its stunning architecture, green spaces, rich history, and cultural events. It's the perfect place for travelers who want to experience something unique and off the beaten path.

GETTING TO LJUBLJANA

Ljubljana is easily accessible by air, rail, or road. The Ljubljana Jože Pučnik Airport is the main international gateway to the city, with regular flights from major European cities. The city is also well-connected by train, with direct connections to Vienna, Munich, Zagreb, and Venice.

EXPLORING THE CITY

The city center of Ljubljana is best explored on foot. The Old Town is a must-visit, with its cobbled streets, colorful buildings, and beautiful architecture. Don't miss the iconic Triple Bridge, the famous Preseren Square, and the Ljubljana Castle, which offers stunning views of the city.

The city's green spaces are also worth exploring. Tivoli Park, located just a short walk from the city center, is a great place for a picnic or a leisurely stroll. The park is also home to the National Museum of Contemporary History and the Tivoli Mansion.

CULTURE AND ENTERTAINMENT

Ljubljana has a rich cultural scene, with many theaters, museums, and galleries. The Ljubljana Opera House is a must-visit for music lovers, while the Museum of Modern Art is a great place to discover the work of Slovenian artists.

The city also hosts many cultural events throughout the year, including the Ljubljana Jazz Festival, the Ljubljana International Film Festival, and the Ljubljana Festival, which features performances by some of the world's top musicians and artists.

FOOD AND DRINK

Slovenian cuisine is a unique blend of Central European and Mediterranean influences. The city's restaurants offer a variety of traditional and modern dishes, with a focus on fresh, local ingredients.

Don't miss the chance to try some of the local specialties, such as the hearty beef stew known as Jota, or the traditional dumplings called Idrijski žlikrofi. Wash it down with a glass of local wine or a cold beer from one of the city's many craft breweries.

FINAL THOUGHTS

Ljubljana is a hidden gem in the heart of Europe, offering travelers a unique blend of history, culture, and natural beauty. Whether you're exploring the city's picturesque streets, enjoying a performance at one of its many cultural events, or sampling the local cuisine, Ljubljana is a destination that should not be missed.

KAZAN, RUSSIA

Kazan is a city located in the Republic of Tatarstan, Russia, and is a melting pot of diverse cultures and traditions. It is a city with a rich history, stunning architecture, and an array of exciting activities and experiences to offer.

GETTING TO KAZAN

Kazan has an international airport, which is well connected to major cities across the world. Alternatively, one can reach Kazan by train, bus, or car from other Russian cities.

HISTORY AND CULTURE

Kazan's history dates back to the 10th century, and the city has witnessed several invasions and wars over the years. The city has managed to preserve its rich cultural heritage, which is evident in the Kazan Kremlin, a UNESCO World Heritage Site, and the Qolşärif Mosque. Other places of historical and cultural significance include the Kazan State University, the Kazan Opera and Ballet Theater, and the Hermitage-Kazan Exhibition Center.

GASTRONOMY

Kazan's cuisine is a fusion of Tatar, Russian, and other Central Asian influences, resulting in a unique culinary experience. The city is famous for dishes such as chak-chak, echpochmak, and qistibi, which are must-tries for any food enthusiast. Visitors can explore the city's culinary delights at the Tatar Cuisine Museum or take a food tour of the city.

EXPLORING KAZAN'S OUTDOORS

Kazan is also a city with plenty of outdoor activities and green spaces. Visitors can take a stroll along the pedestrian street of Bauman or explore the Kazan Riviera, a park that stretches along the Volga River. The city is also home to several parks, such as the Gorky Central Park and the Millennium Park, which offer plenty of recreational activities.

CONCLUSION

Kazan is a city with a unique blend of history, culture, cuisine, and outdoor activities. Whether you are a history buff, food enthusiast, or nature lover, Kazan has something to offer everyone. So, if you are planning a trip to Russia, don't forget to add Kazan to your itinerary.

SPLIT, CROATIA

Split City, also known as Split-Dalmatia, is a popular tourist destination in Croatia. This ancient city boasts a rich history and culture, with influences from the Romans, Venetians, and Austrians. Its unique blend of old and new, together with its scenic beauty, makes it a must-visit destination for travelers.

LOCATION AND HISTORY

Split City is located on the Adriatic coast in the Dalmatian region of Croatia. The city was founded in the fourth century BC by the Greeks, and later occupied by the Romans. The Diocletian Palace, a UNESCO World Heritage site, was built in the fourth century AD and remains the city's most iconic landmark.

OLD TOWN AND DIOCLETIAN PALACE

Split's Old Town is a labyrinth of winding streets and alleys, with charming cafes, shops, and restaurants. The Diocletian Palace is the centerpiece of the Old Town and is one of the best-preserved Roman monuments in the world. Visitors can explore the palace's underground chambers, climb the bell tower for panoramic views of the city, or simply stroll through its courtyards and admire the ancient architecture.

BEACHES AND NATURE

Split City has several beautiful beaches, including Bacvice, Kasjuni, and Znjan. These beaches are perfect for swimming, sunbathing, and water sports. For those seeking adventure, there are also several national parks nearby, including Krka National Park and Plitvice Lakes National Park, which offer hiking, biking, and rafting opportunities.

NIGHTLIFE AND ENTERTAINMENT

Split City has a vibrant nightlife scene, with numerous bars, nightclubs, and live music venues. The Bacvice Beach Club is a popular spot for dancing and socializing, while the Vidilica Cafe offers a more laid-back atmosphere with stunning views of the city. The Split Summer Festival is also held annually, featuring theater, dance, and music performances.

CONCLUSION

Split City is a unique and charming destination that offers something for everyone. Whether you're interested in history, culture, nature, or nightlife, this city has it all. Its ancient architecture, stunning beaches, and vibrant entertainment scene make it a top travel destination in Europe. So, pack your bags and discover the unique charm of Split City for yourself!

GRONINGEN, NETHERLANDS

Groningen is a charming city located in the northern part of the Netherlands. Known for its vibrant energy, stunning architecture, and rich cultural scene, Groningen is a must-visit destination for travelers looking for a unique European experience.

GETTING TO GRONINGEN

The city can be easily accessed by train or bus from major cities in the Netherlands, such as Amsterdam and Rotterdam. The nearest airport is Groningen Airport Eelde, which has direct flights to a few European cities.

DISCOVERING THE CITY CENTER

The city center of Groningen is compact and perfect for exploring on foot or by bicycle. The Martini Tower, a 97-meter high tower, is a prominent landmark in the city and offers stunning views of the surrounding areas. The Grote Markt, the central square of Groningen, is a bustling hub of activity and a great place to soak up the local atmosphere. Visitors can also wander through the historic streets of the city, admiring the unique architecture and charming cafes.

CULTURAL HIGHLIGHTS

Groningen is known for its rich cultural scene, with a variety of museums, galleries, and theaters to explore. The

Groninger Museum, located in a striking modern building, houses a wide range of contemporary art and design exhibitions. The Noorderlicht Photogallery is another must-visit destination for photography enthusiasts. The city also hosts a variety of festivals and events throughout the year, such as the Groningen Noorderzon Performing Arts Festival and the Eurosonic Noorderslag music festival.

CUISINE

Groningen has a vibrant culinary scene, with plenty of options for foodies to explore. The city is known for its traditional Dutch cuisine, such as stamppot (a dish made with mashed potatoes and vegetables) and erwtensoep (pea soup). Visitors can also sample international cuisine, with plenty of restaurants serving Italian, Japanese, and Indonesian dishes.

CONCLUSION

Groningen is a vibrant and charming city with a rich cultural scene, stunning architecture, and delicious cuisine. Whether you're interested in exploring museums and galleries, wandering through historic streets, or simply enjoying a meal at a local restaurant, Groningen has something for everyone.

STRASBOURG, FRANCE

Strasbourg is a charming city located in the eastern part of France, close to the German border. This city, with its stunning architecture, rich history, and vibrant culture, has plenty to offer to visitors. Whether you are a history buff, a food lover, or an art enthusiast, Strasbourg is the perfect destination for a memorable trip.

GETTING TO STRASBOURG

Strasbourg is easily accessible by plane, train, or car. The city is served by Strasbourg International Airport, which has direct flights from major European cities. There are also frequent train connections to Strasbourg from Paris and other major French cities. If you prefer to drive, Strasbourg is easily reachable via the French highway network.

EXPLORING THE OLD TOWN

The heart of Strasbourg is its historic old town, known as the Grande Île. This charming neighborhood is a UNESCO World Heritage Site and is famous for its picturesque streets, beautiful half-timbered houses, and impressive Gothic cathedral. A stroll through the old town is a journey through time, taking you back to the medieval era.

VISITING STRASBOURG CATHEDRAL

One of the must-see attractions in Strasbourg is the stunning Cathedral Notre-Dame de Strasbourg. This Gothic masterpiece is over 1,000 years old and features a remarkable facade, intricate sculptures, and stunning stained-glass windows. Climbing the cathedral's tower is highly recommended as it offers breathtaking views of the city.

ENJOYING THE LOCAL CUISINE

Strasbourg is known for its delicious local cuisine, which combines French and German influences. The city is famous for its sausages, sauerkraut, and flammekueche, a type of thin crust pizza topped with cream, onions, and bacon. There are also many bakeries and patisseries in Strasbourg where you can indulge in mouth-watering pastries, such as macarons and kougelhopf.

EXPLORING THE MUSEUMS

Strasbourg is home to many museums that showcase the city's rich history and culture. The Museum of Fine Arts is a must-see for art lovers, featuring works by renowned artists such as Botticelli and Goya. The Alsatian Museum is another highlight, offering a glimpse into the local traditions and customs of the region.

CONCLUSION

In conclusion, Strasbourg is a fascinating city that offers something for everyone. Whether you are interested in history, culture, or cuisine, Strasbourg is a destination that will leave you enchanted. From its charming old town to its delicious local cuisine, Strasbourg is a city that will capture your heart and leave you with unforgettable memories.

NICOSIA, CYPRUS

Nicosia, the capital city of Cyprus, is a charming destination that offers visitors an unforgettable experience. The city's rich history and cultural diversity make it a must-visit destination for travelers looking for an authentic and immersive experience.

THE OLD TOWN

The Old Town of Nicosia is a labyrinth of narrow alleys and winding streets that will take you back in time. The city's impressive Venetian walls, gates, and bastions are a testament to its past as a strategic stronghold. The Old Town is also home to numerous museums and galleries, showcasing the city's cultural heritage, including the Leventis Municipal Museum, the Cyprus Museum, and the Folk Art Museum.

GREEN SPACES

Nicosia boasts several green spaces that offer a peaceful escape from the city's bustling streets. The city's largest park, the Pedieos River Linear Park, stretches for 15 kilometers along the riverbank, providing a scenic walking and cycling route. Other green spaces include the Athalassa National Forest Park, a serene haven for nature lovers, and the Presidential Palace Gardens, a tranquil oasis in the heart of the city.

CUISINE

Cyprus is known for its delectable cuisine, and Nicosia is no exception. The city is home to a vibrant food scene, offering a range of traditional and modern dishes that will tantalize your taste buds. Meze, a selection of small dishes, is a must-try culinary experience, and there are plenty of restaurants and tavernas in the Old Town that serve this Cypriot specialty.

SHOPPING

Nicosia is a shopper's paradise, with a variety of shopping options to suit every taste and budget. The Old Town is home to traditional souvenir shops, antique stores, and handicraft markets, while the modern shopping malls on the outskirts of the city offer a range of international brands and designer stores.

CONCLUSION

Nicosia is a city that will captivate and enchant you with its history, culture, and charm. Whether you're interested in exploring the city's ancient past, indulging in its culinary delights, or shopping till you drop, Nicosia has something for everyone. Plan your visit today and discover the magic of this hidden gem in the heart of Cyprus.

BERGEN, NORWAY

Bergen is a charming city located on the southwestern coast of Norway, surrounded by mountains and fjords. It is a cultural and historical hub, known for its picturesque views, stunning architecture, and vibrant nightlife. In this article, we will explore the various attractions that make Bergen an ideal destination for travelers.

HISTORIC SITES

One of the main attractions in Bergen is Bryggen, a UNESCO World Heritage Site. It is a group of colorful wooden buildings that date back to the 14th century. Bryggen was a major trading center during the Hanseatic League, and today it houses shops, cafes, and restaurants.

Another historical site worth visiting is the Bergenhus Fortress, which was built in the 13th century to protect the city from enemy attacks. The fortress has several museums, including the Bergenhus Museum, which showcases the city's history.

CULTURAL GEMS

Bergen has a rich cultural scene, with numerous museums, galleries, and theaters. The Bergen Art Museum is home to a vast collection of Norwegian art, while the KODE Art Museums of Bergen has a collection of international art, including works by Pablo Picasso and Edvard Munch.

The Grieghallen concert hall is a popular venue for classical music concerts, and the Den Nationale Scene is the oldest theater in Bergen, showcasing Norwegian plays and performances.

NATURAL BEAUTY

Bergen is surrounded by stunning natural beauty, including seven mountains that offer panoramic views of the city and the fjords. Mount Fløyen is a popular hiking destination, and visitors can take a funicular to the top for breathtaking views.

The Bergen Fish Market is another attraction that should not be missed. It is located near the harbor and offers a wide selection of fresh seafood, including salmon, cod, and shrimp.

FINAL THOUGHTS

Bergen is a beautiful city that offers a unique blend of history, culture, and natural beauty. Whether you're interested in exploring the city's historic sites, cultural gems, or natural wonders, there is something for everyone in Bergen. It is a must-visit destination for travelers looking for an unforgettable experience.

LUXEMBOURG CITY, LUXEMBOURG

Luxembourg City, the capital of the Grand Duchy of Luxembourg, is a charming and historic city located in the heart of Europe. With its picturesque old town, impressive fortifications, and lively cultural scene, it's no wonder that the city has become a popular destination for travelers from all over the world.

EXPLORING THE OLD TOWN

The old town of Luxembourg City, also known as the "Ville Haute," is a UNESCO World Heritage site and one of the main attractions of the city. Here you'll find narrow cobblestone streets, charming cafes, and historic buildings, including the impressive Grand Ducal Palace. Be sure to also visit the Bock Casemates, a network of tunnels and chambers carved into the city's rock fortifications, which offer stunning views of the city below.

A CULTURAL HUB

Luxembourg City is also home to a thriving cultural scene. The city boasts numerous museums and galleries, including the Luxembourg City History Museum, the Museum of Modern Art, and the National Museum of Natural History. The Philharmonie Luxembourg, one of Europe's most renowned concert halls, offers a diverse program of classical, jazz, and world music concerts throughout the year.

OUTDOOR ACTIVITIES

For those who love the outdoors, Luxembourg City offers plenty of opportunities for hiking, cycling, and exploring the city's beautiful parks and gardens. The Pétrusse Valley Park, located in the heart of the city, is a popular destination for picnics and leisurely walks, while the nearby Ardennes region offers more challenging hikes and outdoor adventures.

CONCLUSION

Luxembourg City may be small in size, but it offers a wealth of attractions and activities for travelers of all interests. With its rich history, vibrant cultural scene, and stunning natural surroundings, it's no wonder that Luxembourg City has become a must-visit destination for anyone exploring Europe.

VIGO, SPAIN

Vigo City is a charming port city located in the northwest region of Spain. It is situated on the coast of the Atlantic Ocean and is known for its beautiful beaches, delicious seafood, and vibrant nightlife. The city is a perfect destination for travelers looking to experience the rich history and culture of Spain while also enjoying the beautiful scenery.

EXPLORING THE OLD TOWN

The old town of Vigo is a must-see destination for any traveler. It is a picturesque neighborhood with narrow streets, small squares, and beautiful buildings. You can explore the old town on foot, taking in the architecture and history of the city. There are plenty of cafes and restaurants in the area, so you can stop and enjoy a meal or a drink while taking in the sights.

RELAXING ON THE BEACH

Vigo is famous for its beaches, and there are plenty of them to choose from. The most popular is Samil Beach, which is a beautiful, long stretch of white sand. You can relax on the beach, swim in the ocean, or try your hand at some water sports. If you're looking for a quieter spot, you can head to one of the smaller, more secluded beaches in the area.

ENJOYING THE LOCAL CUISINE

One of the highlights of visiting Vigo is trying the local cuisine. As a coastal city, Vigo is known for its seafood, and you'll find plenty of delicious options on the menu. You can try the local specialty, octopus, or sample some of the fresh fish that is caught daily in the Atlantic Ocean. Don't forget to try some of the local wines and spirits while you're there, too.

EXPERIENCING THE NIGHTLIFE

Vigo has a vibrant nightlife, with plenty of bars and clubs to choose from. You can start the evening with a drink at a local bar, then dance the night away at one of the city's clubs. The nightlife scene in Vigo is lively and diverse, with something for everyone.

FINAL THOUGHTS

Vigo City is a beautiful destination that offers something for everyone. Whether you're interested in history, culture, food, or nightlife, you'll find plenty to enjoy in this charming city. So why not book your trip today and discover the beauty of Vigo for yourself?

KAUNAS, LITHUANIA

Lithuania, located in the heart of Europe, is a country rich in history, culture, and natural beauty. One of its lesser-known but equally fascinating destinations is Kaunas, the country's second-largest city. With its picturesque Old Town, stunning architecture, and lively arts and entertainment scene, Kaunas is a hidden gem that's worth a visit.

A RICH HISTORY

Kaunas has a rich and complex history that spans centuries. The city was first mentioned in written records in the 14th century, and it has been inhabited since prehistoric times. Over the years, Kaunas has been ruled by various powers, including the Teutonic Order, the Grand Duchy of Lithuania, the Russian Empire, and the Soviet Union. Each of these periods has left its mark on the city's architecture, culture, and identity.

OLD TOWN CHARM

The heart of Kaunas is its charming Old Town, a maze of cobbled streets and colorful buildings that date back to the Middle Ages. The Old Town is home to a number of historic landmarks, including the Gothic-style Kaunas Castle, the impressive Town Hall, and the stunning St. George's Church. It's a perfect place to wander around and soak up the atmosphere.

ART AND CULTURE

Kaunas is a city with a vibrant arts and entertainment scene. The city is home to several museums, including the impressive M. K. Čiurlionis National Art Museum, which showcases the works of the famous Lithuanian composer and artist. There are also numerous galleries, theaters, and music venues, as well as a bustling nightlife that caters to all tastes.

GREEN SPACES

Kaunas is a city that loves its green spaces. The city is home to a number of parks and gardens, including the beautiful Pazaislis Monastery Park, which features a stunning baroque church and a tranquil lake. The city's largest park, Nemunas Island, is a popular destination for walkers, joggers, and cyclists, and it offers stunning views of the Nemunas River.

FOOD AND DRINK

Kaunas is a city that knows how to eat and drink well. Lithuanian cuisine is hearty and delicious, and there are plenty of restaurants and cafes in Kaunas that serve traditional dishes like cepelinai (potato dumplings filled with meat or cheese), kugelis (potato pudding), and saltibarsciai (cold beet soup). The city also has a thriving craft beer scene, with several breweries producing top-quality beers.

IN CONCLUSION

Kaunas may not be as well-known as some of Europe's other great cities, but it is a destination that is well worth discovering. With its rich history, charming Old Town, vibrant arts and entertainment scene, green spaces, and delicious cuisine, Kaunas has something for everyone. If you're planning a trip to Lithuania, make sure to add Kaunas to your itinerary.

BRISTOL, ENGLAND

Bristol is a charming city located in the southwest of England. It is a city full of surprises, with a rich history, vibrant culture, and a lively nightlife scene. From its beautiful parks and historic landmarks to its modern art scene and diverse cuisine, Bristol has something for everyone.

HISTORY AND CULTURE

Bristol has a fascinating history that dates back to the Roman era. The city played a significant role in the slave trade in the 18th century and was heavily bombed during World War II. Today, visitors can explore the city's history by visiting museums such as the Bristol Museum & Art Gallery, the M Shed, and the SS Great Britain. The city is also home to a vibrant arts scene, with numerous galleries, theaters, and music venues that showcase local and international talent.

ATTRACTIONS AND LANDMARKS

Bristol is home to several landmarks and attractions that are worth visiting. The Clifton Suspension Bridge is one of the city's most iconic landmarks and offers stunning views of the Avon Gorge. Another must-see attraction is the Bristol Zoo Gardens, which is home to over 400 species of animals. Visitors can also explore the city's beautiful parks, such as Brandon Hill and Queen Square.

FOOD AND DRINK

Bristol has a thriving food and drink scene that is sure to impress any foodie. The city is home to a range of restaurants, cafes, and bars that offer everything from traditional British cuisine to international flavors. The St. Nicholas Market is a must-visit for food lovers, with numerous stalls selling fresh produce, artisanal cheeses, and exotic spices.

NIGHTLIFE

Bristol has a lively nightlife scene, with numerous bars, clubs, and music venues that cater to all tastes. The city is particularly famous for its music scene, with a vibrant underground scene that has produced numerous successful artists. Some of the city's most popular venues include Thekla, The Fleece, and the O2 Academy.

CONCLUSION

Bristol is a city full of surprises and is sure to delight visitors of all ages. With its rich history, vibrant culture, and lively nightlife scene, there is always something to see and do in this charming city. Whether you're a history buff, a foodie, or a music lover, Bristol has something for everyone.

SALZBURG, AUSTRIA

Salzburg, located in western Austria, is a city that boasts both cultural and scenic marvels. The city, with its history, architecture, and natural beauty, has something to offer for every kind of traveler. Salzburg is famous for its classical music scene, its baroque architecture, and as the birthplace of the legendary composer Wolfgang Amadeus Mozart.

THE OLD TOWN

The Old Town of Salzburg, also known as Altstadt, is a UNESCO World Heritage Site and a hub of the city's cultural heritage. The town features narrow streets, historic buildings, and an array of architectural wonders. The DomQuartier Salzburg, located in the heart of the Old Town, is a must-visit. It is an exquisite collection of museums, galleries, and palaces that showcases the city's rich cultural heritage.

CITY OF MUSIC

Salzburg is known as the city of music, and for a good reason. The city has a rich tradition of classical music and is home to the famous Salzburg Festival. The festival, held annually in July and August, attracts music lovers from all over the world. The festival features classical music concerts, opera performances, and theater shows.

NATURAL BEAUTY

Salzburg is situated on the banks of the Salzach River, surrounded by the majestic Alps. The city offers plenty of opportunities for outdoor activities, such as hiking, biking, and skiing. The Salzburg Zoo, located at the foot of the Hellbrunn Mountain, is a popular attraction for families.

CULINARY DELIGHTS

Salzburg is renowned for its culinary delights, such as the Salzburger Nockerl, a sweet soufflé dessert, and the Mozartkugel, a chocolate treat with a marzipan center. The city has a range of cafes, restaurants, and bars that offer traditional Austrian cuisine and international dishes.

CONCLUSION

Salzburg is a unique blend of history, culture, and natural beauty. The city is a must-visit for anyone interested in classical music, architecture, and outdoor activities. The city's Old Town, music scene, natural beauty, and culinary delights make it a perfect destination for a memorable vacation.

CÓRDOBA, SPAIN

If you're looking for a charming and historic city to explore in Spain, Córdoba is a must-visit destination. Located in the southern region of Andalusia, this city is home to a rich cultural and architectural heritage that is sure to captivate visitors.

GETTING TO CÓRDOBA

The city is easily accessible by train from Madrid or Seville, and there are also direct flights to the nearby city of Seville. Once you arrive, you can explore the city on foot or by renting a bike.

HISTORY AND CULTURE

Córdoba's history dates back to the Roman Empire, and its strategic location made it a center of Islamic learning and culture during the Middle Ages. One of the city's most famous landmarks is the Mezquita-Catedral, a stunning mosque-cathedral that is a testament to the city's diverse cultural influences.

In addition to the Mezquita-Catedral, visitors can explore the Alcázar de los Reyes Cristianos, a medieval castle that was once the residence of the Catholic monarchs. The city also boasts a number of museums, including the Museum of Fine Arts and the Archaeological Museum.

CULINARY DELIGHTS

Córdoba is known for its delicious cuisine, which blends traditional Spanish flavors with influences from the Middle East and North Africa. Some of the city's most famous dishes include salmorejo, a cold tomato soup, and rabo de toro, a slow-cooked oxtail stew.

Visitors can sample these dishes and more at the city's numerous tapas bars and restaurants. Be sure to wash it all down with a glass of local wine or sherry.

NIGHTLIFE

After a day of exploring the city's sights and sounds, visitors can unwind and enjoy the nightlife in Córdoba. The city boasts a vibrant music scene, with live performances of traditional flamenco music and dance.

There are also plenty of bars and nightclubs where you can dance the night away to the latest pop hits or enjoy a drink with friends.

CONCLUSION

Córdoba is a hidden gem in the heart of Andalusia, and a city that should be on any traveler's bucket list. With its rich history, delicious cuisine, and vibrant nightlife, there is something for everyone in this charming Spanish city.

ZAGREB, CROATIA

Zagreb is the capital and largest city of Croatia, located in the northwestern part of the country. This historic city has a lot to offer for travelers seeking a mix of old-world charm and modern amenities. Let's explore some of the highlights of this captivating destination.

GETTING TO ZAGREB

Zagreb is easily accessible by air, train, and bus. The city's international airport, Franjo Tuđman Airport, is only a 20-minute drive from the city center. You can also take a train or bus from other Croatian cities or neighboring countries like Slovenia, Serbia, and Austria.

HISTORIC OLD TOWN

Zagreb's old town, known as Gornji Grad, is a must-visit for history and architecture buffs. The area is home to many historic buildings and landmarks, such as the Zagreb Cathedral, St. Mark's Church, and the Stone Gate. Take a stroll along the charming cobblestone streets and marvel at the colorful facades of the Baroque-style buildings.

LOCAL CUISINE

Croatian cuisine is a blend of Mediterranean and Central European flavors, and Zagreb offers plenty of opportunities to savor the local dishes. Be sure to try traditional dishes like Peka, a slow-cooked meat and vegetable dish, or Ćevapi, grilled minced meat served with flatbread and onions. For dessert, sample a slice of Kremšnita, a creamy vanilla custard cake that is a local favorite.

VIBRANT CULTURE

Zagreb has a lively cultural scene, with many museums, galleries, and theaters to explore. The Croatian Museum of Naive Art showcases the works of self-taught artists, while the Museum of Broken Relationships is a unique display of objects and stories from failed relationships. The Croatian National Theatre and the Vatroslav Lisinski Concert Hall are both great venues to catch a performance.

PARKS AND GREEN SPACES

Zagreb is home to many parks and green spaces, providing a welcome respite from the hustle and bustle of the city. Maksimir Park, located in the eastern part of the city, is the oldest public park in Croatia and features a zoo, lakes, and numerous walking trails. The Botanical Garden is another must-visit, with over 10,000 plant species from around the world.

CONCLUSION

Zagreb is a fascinating destination that offers a perfect blend of history, culture, and natural beauty. Whether you're interested in exploring the city's historic old town, sampling the local cuisine, or simply relaxing in one of its many parks, Zagreb is sure to captivate and delight.

TURKU, FINLAND

Located on the southwest coast of Finland, Turku is the country's oldest city and boasts a rich history and cultural heritage that is sure to captivate visitors from around the world. From its charming cobblestone streets to its stunning archipelago, Turku has something for everyone.

GETTING TO TURKU

Turku is easily accessible by plane, train, or bus. The Turku Airport is located just outside the city center and serves several international airlines. Alternatively, you can take a train or bus from Helsinki, which takes approximately two hours.

EXPLORING THE CITY CENTER

Turku's city center is home to numerous landmarks and attractions that are worth visiting. Start your journey at the Turku Cathedral, a Gothic masterpiece that dates back to the 13th century. Next, head to the Turku Castle, which was founded in the late 13th century and served as a residence for Finnish royalty for centuries. Visitors can take guided tours of the castle and learn about its fascinating history.

CULTURAL ATTRACTIONS

In addition to its historical landmarks, Turku is also home to several museums and cultural institutions that celebrate Finnish art and culture. The Turku Art Museum is a must-visit for art lovers, showcasing works from both Finnish and international artists. The Museum of History and Contemporary Art, on the other hand, focuses on Finnish history and features exhibitions on topics ranging from the Stone Age to modern times.

OUTDOOR ADVENTURES

For those who love the great outdoors, Turku has plenty to offer. The city is situated on the shores of the Baltic Sea and is home to a stunning archipelago that is perfect for boating and island hopping. Visitors can also explore the city's many parks and green spaces, including the Turku Botanic Garden and the Kupittaa Park, which features walking trails, a playground, and a small amusement park.

CONCLUSION

With its rich history, vibrant culture, and natural beauty, Turku is a city that has something for everyone. Whether you're interested in exploring the city's landmarks and museums, or you prefer outdoor adventures, Turku is a destination that is sure to leave a lasting impression. So, the next time you're planning a trip to Finland, be sure to add Turku to your itinerary!

AALBORG, DENMARK

Located in northern Denmark, Aalborg is a charming city with a rich history and vibrant culture. With its mix of modern architecture and historic buildings, bustling streets, and scenic waterfront, Aalborg has something to offer for everyone.

GETTING AROUND

The best way to explore Aalborg is on foot or by bike. The city is relatively small and easy to navigate, with plenty of pedestrian-only areas and bike lanes. If you prefer public transportation, buses and trains are also available.

ATTRACTIONS

Aalborg is home to several notable attractions, including the Aalborg Zoo, which is home to more than 100 different animal species. The Aalborg Tower, which offers panoramic views of the city and surrounding area, is another popular spot for visitors.

For those interested in history, Aalborg's Old Town is a must-see. The area is filled with picturesque cobblestone streets, historic buildings, and quaint shops and cafes. The Aalborg Historical Museum, located in the heart of the Old Town, provides a glimpse into the city's past, from the Viking era to the present day.

CULTURE AND ENTERTAINMENT

Aalborg is known for its vibrant cultural scene. The city hosts several festivals throughout the year, including the Aalborg Carnival, which attracts thousands of visitors from around the world. The city is also home to several theaters, museums, and galleries, showcasing both local and international art and culture.

FOOD AND DRINK

Aalborg is a food lover's paradise, with plenty of restaurants, cafes, and bars serving up a variety of local and international cuisine. The city is known for its seafood, and visitors can enjoy everything from fresh fish and shellfish to traditional Danish dishes like smørrebrød.

NIGHTLIFE

Aalborg has a lively nightlife scene, with plenty of bars, clubs, and pubs to choose from. The Jomfru Ane Gade is a popular street lined with bars and nightclubs, making it a hub for partygoers.

CONCLUSION

Aalborg is a charming city that is rich in culture and history. Whether you're interested in exploring the city's attractions, trying the local cuisine, or experiencing its vibrant nightlife, Aalborg has something to offer for everyone.

GAZIANTEP, TURKEY

Gaziantep, a city located in the southeast of Turkey, is a cultural and historical hub that offers visitors an unforgettable experience. With its vibrant bazaars, mouth-watering cuisine, and rich history, Gaziantep has something to offer for everyone.

HISTORY AND CULTURE

Gaziantep is a city steeped in history and culture. It is home to numerous historical landmarks, including the Gaziantep Castle, a fortified structure built by the Romans in the 2nd century AD. Another must-see historical site is the Zeugma Mosaic Museum, which boasts an extensive collection of ancient Roman mosaics.

For those interested in experiencing Gaziantep's local culture, the city has several museums that showcase its rich heritage. The Gaziantep Museum of Archaeology, for instance, displays artifacts from the city's ancient past, including Hittite and Roman-era relics.

CUISINE

Gaziantep's cuisine is famous throughout Turkey and the world. The city is known for its delicious baklava, which is made with thin layers of phyllo pastry, chopped nuts, and sweet syrup. Other popular dishes include kebabs, pistachio-based sweets, and locally grown apricots.

BAZAARS

Gaziantep is a paradise for shoppers, with its colorful bazaars and markets selling everything from spices and textiles to jewelry and antiques. The city's most famous bazaar, the Zincirli Bedesten, is a covered market that dates back to the 16th century. Visitors can wander through its winding alleyways and admire the intricate craftsmanship of the goods on offer.

CONCLUSION

Gaziantep is a must-visit destination for those interested in experiencing Turkey's rich history and culture. With its impressive landmarks, mouth-watering cuisine, and bustling bazaars, it is a city that offers visitors a truly unique and unforgettable experience.

BERN, SWITZERLAND

If you're planning a trip to Switzerland, don't miss out on the charming city of Bern. With its cobbled streets, historic architecture, and beautiful river, Bern has a lot to offer visitors. Here's a guide to help you make the most of your visit.

GETTING TO BERN

Bern is easily accessible by train, with direct connections to major cities like Zurich, Geneva, and Basel. The city also has an airport with regular flights to and from several European destinations.

EXPLORING THE OLD TOWN

The heart of Bern is its picturesque Old Town, a UNESCO World Heritage Site. Stroll through its cobblestone streets, marvel at the ornate fountains, and admire the well-preserved medieval architecture. Don't miss the famous Clock Tower, which features an impressive mechanical clock with moving figures.

VISITING MUSEUMS AND GALLERIES

Bern has plenty of museums and galleries to satisfy any cultural craving. The Bern Historical Museum offers a fascinating look at the city's past, while the Kunstmuseum Bern houses an impressive collection of modern and contemporary art. For something a little different, check out the Zentrum Paul Klee, which showcases the works of the Swiss artist of the same name.

ENJOYING NATURE

Bern is blessed with natural beauty, and there are plenty of opportunities to enjoy the great outdoors. Take a stroll along the Aare River, which flows through the city and offers stunning views of the surrounding landscape. If you're feeling adventurous, take a hike in the nearby Gurten Park or take a scenic train ride up to the Bernese Alps.

SAVORING SWISS CUISINE

No trip to Switzerland is complete without trying the local cuisine. Bern has plenty of restaurants and cafes offering traditional Swiss dishes like fondue, raclette, and rösti. Don't forget to try the city's famous almond croissants, which are said to be the best in the country.

CONCLUSION

From its charming Old Town to its stunning natural surroundings, Bern has something to offer everyone. Whether you're a history buff, an art lover, or simply looking for a relaxing getaway, this Swiss gem is not to be missed.

NOVI SAD, SERBIA

When it comes to travel destinations, Europe is a continent that boasts numerous stunning locations. However, one city that often gets overlooked is Novi Sad, Serbia's second-largest city. Situated on the banks of the Danube River, this city offers a unique blend of history, culture, and modernity.

HISTORY AND CULTURE

Novi Sad has a rich history that dates back to the Roman Empire, and evidence of its past can be seen throughout the city. One of the most iconic landmarks is the Petrovaradin Fortress, built in the 17th century. Today, the fortress is a popular tourist spot, offering stunning views of the city and the Danube River. Visitors can also explore the underground tunnels that once served as military barracks and storage rooms.

Another must-visit destination is the Museum of Vojvodina, which showcases the history and culture of the Vojvodina region, where Novi Sad is located. The museum has an extensive collection of artifacts, including ancient coins, traditional costumes, and artwork.

FESTIVALS AND EVENTS

Novi Sad is known for its lively festivals and events, making it a vibrant city to visit throughout the year. One of the most famous festivals is the Exit Festival, which takes place in July and features world-renowned musicians and artists. The festival takes place at the Petrovaradin Fortress, offering a unique backdrop for live music.

Another popular event is the Novi Sad Jazz Festival, which takes place in November and attracts jazz lovers from all over the world. The festival features performances by renowned jazz musicians and offers a variety of events, including workshops and lectures.

FOOD AND DRINK

Serbian cuisine is hearty and flavorful, and Novi Sad is no exception. Visitors can sample traditional dishes such as cevapi, a grilled minced meat dish, or sarma, a stuffed cabbage roll. The city also has a thriving cafe culture, with numerous cafes and bars offering a relaxed atmosphere to enjoy a cup of coffee or a glass of local wine.

CONCLUSION

Novi Sad is a hidden gem that offers visitors a unique blend of history, culture, and modernity. From its iconic landmarks to its lively festivals and delicious cuisine, there's something for everyone in this vibrant city. So, if you're planning a trip to Europe, make sure to add Novi Sad to your list of must-visit destinations.

STIRLING, SCOTLAND

Stirling is a beautiful city located in central Scotland, known for its rich history and stunning scenery. The city is a popular tourist destination, offering a range of activities that appeal to all ages and interests. Whether you are interested in exploring the historical landmarks, enjoying the scenic views or indulging in some outdoor adventures, Stirling has something for everyone.

HISTORY AND LANDMARKS

Stirling is a city steeped in history, and there are plenty of historical landmarks and attractions to explore. The most notable of these is Stirling Castle, a well-preserved fortress that dates back to the 15th and 16th centuries. The castle sits on top of a hill overlooking the city, offering breathtaking views of the surrounding landscape. Other historical landmarks include the Church of the Holy Rude, the Old Town Jail and the Bannockburn Heritage Centre.

SCENIC VIEWS

Stirling is home to some of the most breathtaking scenery in Scotland. The city is surrounded by rolling hills and lush green countryside, offering stunning views at every turn. One of the best places to enjoy the views is the Wallace Monument, a towering monument dedicated to the Scottish hero William Wallace. The monument offers spectacular views of the city and surrounding countryside from the top.

OUTDOOR ADVENTURES

For those who enjoy outdoor activities, Stirling is the perfect destination. The city is surrounded by several beautiful parks and nature reserves, including the Loch Lomond and The Trossachs National Park. Visitors can enjoy hiking, cycling, fishing and other outdoor activities in these beautiful natural settings. The city also has a range of golf courses and sports facilities, making it a great destination for sports enthusiasts.

FINAL THOUGHTS

Stirling is a city with something for everyone. Whether you are interested in history, nature, or outdoor activities, you will find plenty to keep you entertained. With its stunning scenery, rich history and welcoming locals, Stirling is a must-visit destination for anyone exploring Scotland. So, pack your bags and get ready to discover the beauty of Stirling!

BILBAO, SPAIN

Bilbao is a charming city located in northern Spain, in the Basque Country region. This city has become a popular tourist destination due to its unique blend of modern and traditional architecture, cultural attractions, and culinary scene. Whether you are a history buff, an art lover, or a foodie, Bilbao has something to offer for everyone.

EXPLORE THE OLD TOWN

The old town of Bilbao, known as Casco Viejo, is a must-visit area for tourists. This neighborhood is full of narrow alleys, charming squares, and historic buildings. Walking through the old town, visitors can admire the Gothic-style Santiago Cathedral, which dates back to the 14th century. The Plaza Nueva is another highlight of the area, known for its bustling atmosphere and numerous bars and restaurants.

EXPERIENCE THE GUGGENHEIM MUSEUM

The Guggenheim Museum is one of Bilbao's most iconic landmarks, designed by the renowned architect Frank Gehry. This museum is dedicated to contemporary art and has an impressive collection of works by artists such as Andy Warhol, Jeff Koons, and Eduardo Chillida. Even if you are not an art enthusiast, the building itself is worth a visit, with its unique titanium exterior and stunning interior.

INDULGE IN THE CULINARY SCENE

Bilbao is known for its excellent gastronomy, with a variety of traditional and modern dishes to choose from. Some of the must-try dishes include pintxos, small tapas-style bites usually served on bread, and bacalao al pil-pil, a dish made with salt cod, olive oil, and garlic. The city has a lively food scene, with numerous restaurants, cafes, and bars to choose from.

ENJOY THE OUTDOORS

Bilbao is surrounded by beautiful natural landscapes, perfect for outdoor activities such as hiking and cycling. The nearby Basque Coast is known for its stunning beaches and picturesque fishing villages, such as Getxo and Bermeo. The city also has several parks and gardens, such as the Dona Casilda Iturrizar park, perfect for a relaxing stroll.

IN CONCLUSION

Bilbao is a city that offers a unique mix of culture, art, history, and gastronomy. With its friendly locals and stunning landscapes, it is a destination that is sure to leave a lasting impression on visitors. Whether you are looking for a weekend getaway or a longer vacation, Bilbao is definitely worth a visit.

BANJA LUKA, BOSNIA AND HERZEGOVINA

Nestled in the heart of Bosnia and Herzegovina, Banja Luka is a city that is often overlooked by tourists. However, this hidden gem has a lot to offer visitors who are looking for an authentic Bosnian experience.

HISTORY AND CULTURE

Banja Luka has a rich history that dates back to the Roman Empire. Over the centuries, the city has been ruled by various empires, including the Ottoman Empire and the Austro-Hungarian Empire. Today, visitors can still see the influence of these empires in the city's architecture and culture.

One of the most popular cultural attractions in Banja Luka is the Kastel Fortress, which was built by the Romans in the 2nd century. The fortress has been restored and now houses a museum and art gallery.

Another must-see cultural attraction is the Ferhadija Mosque, which was built in the 16th century during the Ottoman Empire. The mosque was destroyed during the Bosnian War, but has since been rebuilt.

NATURAL BEAUTY

In addition to its rich history and culture, Banja Luka is also known for its natural beauty. The city is surrounded by mountains and is situated on the Vrbas River, making it an ideal destination for outdoor enthusiasts.

One of the most popular outdoor activities in Banja Luka is rafting on the Vrbas River. Visitors can also hike in the nearby mountains, go fishing, or simply enjoy a picnic by the river.

FOOD AND DRINK

No trip to Banja Luka is complete without trying the local cuisine. The city is known for its delicious traditional Bosnian dishes, such as cevapi (grilled minced meat), burek (a savory pastry), and baklava (a sweet pastry).

Visitors can also sample the local beer, Banjalucko, which is brewed in the city. For those who prefer wine, the nearby town of Trebinje is known for its vineyards and wineries.

CONCLUSION

Banja Luka may be a hidden gem, but it has a lot to offer visitors who are looking for an authentic Bosnian experience. With its rich history, natural beauty, and delicious cuisine, Banja Luka is a destination that should not be missed.

STAVANGER, NORWAY

Stavanger Luka, located on the southwest coast of Norway, is a picturesque city that has a lot to offer for travelers looking for a unique and enjoyable vacation. With its stunning natural landscapes, charming historical buildings, and vibrant culture, Stavanger Luka has become a popular destination for tourists from all around the world.

HISTORY AND CULTURE

Stavanger Luka has a rich history that dates back to the Viking Age. The city was founded in the 12th century, and over the centuries, it has become a hub for trade and commerce. Today, Stavanger Luka is known for its thriving arts and culture scene, with numerous museums, galleries, and performance spaces showcasing the city's diverse cultural heritage.

OUTDOOR ADVENTURES

For those who love outdoor activities, Stavanger Luka offers an abundance of opportunities. The city is situated on the coast, providing easy access to water sports like kayaking, sailing, and fishing. There are also several hiking trails and nature parks in the surrounding area, such as the famous Pulpit Rock, which offers stunning views of the fjord below.

FOOD AND DRINK

Stavanger Luka is also a food lover's paradise. The city is famous for its fresh seafood, with several restaurants serving up delicious and authentic Norwegian dishes. Visitors can also enjoy local craft beers, spirits, and wines, as well as specialty coffee shops and bakeries.

SHOPPING AND NIGHTLIFE

In addition to its outdoor activities, Stavanger Luka also offers a variety of shopping and nightlife options. Visitors can browse local markets and boutiques for unique souvenirs and gifts, or enjoy a night out on the town at one of the many bars, clubs, or live music venues.

FINAL THOUGHTS

Overall, Stavanger Luka is a hidden gem that offers something for everyone. Whether you're a nature lover, a history buff, or a foodie, this charming Norwegian city has it all. With its stunning landscapes, rich culture, and friendly locals, Stavanger Luka is the perfect destination for your next vacation.

GRAZ, AUSTRIA

Graz is a charming city located in Austria, with a rich history and culture. The city has been awarded the title of "City of Design" by UNESCO and boasts a vibrant arts and cultural scene. Graz has plenty to offer to visitors, from historic architecture to stunning natural landscapes, making it an ideal destination for travelers looking for a mix of history, culture, and adventure.

HISTORY AND ARCHITECTURE

Graz has a rich history dating back to the Roman times. The city's historical architecture reflects its various influences over the centuries, from Gothic to Renaissance, Baroque, and Art Nouveau. One of the must-visit landmarks in Graz is the Schlossberg, a hill that offers panoramic views of the city and is home to the Clock Tower, a remnant of the city's medieval fortifications.

CULTURE AND ART

Graz has a vibrant arts and cultural scene, with numerous museums and galleries showcasing the works of local and international artists. The city is home to the Kunsthaus Graz, a futuristic art museum designed by Peter Cook and Colin Fournier, which features contemporary art exhibitions. Visitors can also explore the Universalmuseum Joanneum, which includes several museums showcasing the city's history, art, and culture.

CULINARY DELIGHTS

Graz is also known for its delicious culinary offerings, with a variety of traditional and modern restaurants, cafes, and bars. The city's traditional cuisine includes dishes such as the Styrian fried chicken, pumpkin seed oil, and the famous Styrian wine. Visitors can enjoy a wide range of culinary experiences in Graz, from fine dining to street food, all with a distinct Austrian flavor.

NATURAL BEAUTY

Graz is surrounded by stunning natural landscapes, including the Schöckl mountain and the Graz Forest. These natural wonders provide opportunities for outdoor activities such as hiking, mountain biking, and skiing. Visitors can also explore the Mur River, which runs through the city, offering scenic views and opportunities for water sports.

FINAL THOUGHTS

Graz is a fascinating city with a rich history, culture, and culinary scene, and it offers a unique travel experience for visitors. From its historic landmarks to its modern art and culture, the city has something to offer to everyone. Whether you're a foodie, an outdoor enthusiast, or a history buff, Graz is a destination worth exploring.

ODENSE, DENMARK

Odense, located in the center of Denmark's Funen Island, is a vibrant and historic city that has been attracting visitors for centuries. With its charming streets, picturesque architecture, and rich cultural heritage, Odense is the perfect destination for those who want to explore the heart of Denmark. Here's a closer look at what makes this city so special.

HISTORY AND CULTURE

Odense is best known as the birthplace of Hans Christian Andersen, the famous fairy tale writer. The city is filled with tributes to Andersen, including the Hans Christian Andersen Museum and the bronze statue of him in the town square. In addition to Andersen, Odense has a rich cultural history that includes Viking settlements, medieval castles, and a thriving arts scene. Visitors can explore the city's museums, galleries, and theaters to get a taste of the local culture.

ATTRACTIONS

There are many attractions in Odense that appeal to a wide range of interests. For history buffs, the Odense Castle and the Funen Village are must-see destinations. The Odense Zoo, which is home to over 2,000 animals from around the world, is a great place to take the kids. For those who love the outdoors, the Fruens Bøge forest and the Odense River are perfect for hiking and biking.

FOOD AND DRINK

Odense is known for its delicious food and drink, including fresh seafood, locally brewed beer, and traditional Danish pastries. Visitors can explore the city's markets, cafes, and restaurants to sample the local cuisine. One popular dish is the "smørrebrød," a traditional Danish open-faced sandwich that can be topped with everything from smoked salmon to pickled herring.

GETTING AROUND

Odense is a very walkable city, with many of its attractions located within a short distance of each other. Visitors can also rent bikes or take the city's public transportation system, which includes buses and trains. The city is well-connected to other parts of Denmark, making it easy to explore the surrounding areas.

CONCLUSION

Odense is a wonderful destination for those who want to experience the best of Denmark. With its rich history, vibrant culture, and beautiful attractions, there is something for everyone in this charming city. Whether you are traveling solo, with friends, or with family, Odense is a must-visit destination.

LINZ, AUSTRIA

Nestled on the banks of the Danube River, Linz is a charming city in Austria that boasts a perfect mix of history, culture, and innovation. With its beautifully preserved old town, world-renowned museums, and vibrant cultural scene, Linz is a destination that will satisfy any traveler's interests.

EXPLORING THE OLD TOWN

Linz's Old Town is a must-visit for any traveler who wants to experience the city's rich history and architectural beauty. The narrow streets, colorful houses, and baroque buildings give the area a fairy-tale-like ambiance. The Hauptplatz, the city's main square, is lined with historic buildings and is a perfect spot to take in the city's ambiance.

ART AND CULTURE

Linz is a hub for the arts and culture in Austria, with world-class museums, galleries, and theaters. The Lentos Museum of Modern Art is one of the city's top attractions, showcasing a vast collection of contemporary art. The Ars Electronica Center, located on the banks of the Danube River, is another popular destination for those interested in cutting-edge technology and art.

INNOVATION AND SCIENCE

Linz is also known for its innovative spirit, which is evident in the city's state-of-the-art technology and research centers. The voestalpine steel plant, located on the outskirts of the city, is one of the most advanced steel production facilities in the world. The Johannes Kepler University Linz, one of Austria's leading research institutions, is another testament to the city's commitment to innovation.

CULINARY DELIGHTS

No trip to Linz is complete without indulging in some of the city's culinary delights. Linz's cuisine is a unique blend of traditional Austrian fare and modern influences. The city is known for its delicious Linzer Torte, a pastry made with almond flour and raspberry jam. The Pöstlingbergbahn, a historic tram, takes visitors up to the Pöstlingberg mountain, where they can enjoy stunning views of the city while savoring some of the best traditional Austrian dishes.

CONCLUSION

Linz is a city that offers something for everyone, whether you're interested in history, art, technology, or cuisine. Its perfect blend of tradition and modernity makes it a unique and unforgettable destination. So, next time you plan a trip to Austria, be sure to include Linz in your itinerary.

VARNA, BULGARIA

Varna is a picturesque city located on the Black Sea coast of Bulgaria. With its rich cultural heritage, stunning beaches, and vibrant nightlife, it's no wonder that Varna has become a popular destination for travelers seeking a mix of relaxation and excitement.

GETTING THERE

Varna has its own international airport, making it easily accessible from anywhere in the world. Alternatively, visitors can take a bus or train from other cities in Bulgaria or neighboring countries such as Romania or Turkey.

CULTURE AND HISTORY

Varna is one of the oldest cities in Europe, with a history that dates back more than 5,000 years. Visitors can explore ancient ruins such as the Roman baths and the

Thracian Necropolis, which is a UNESCO World Heritage site. The city also has several museums and art galleries, showcasing Bulgarian history and contemporary art.

BEACHES AND NATURE

Varna is home to some of the most beautiful beaches in Bulgaria, with crystal-clear waters and golden sand. The most popular beaches include Golden Sands and Albena, both of which offer a wide range of water sports and beach activities. Visitors can also explore the nearby nature reserves and parks, such as the Varna Ecopark or the Kamchia Biosphere Reserve.

NIGHTLIFE AND ENTERTAINMENT

Varna is known for its lively nightlife, with plenty of bars, clubs, and restaurants to choose from. Visitors can enjoy a night out at the Sea Garden, a popular promenade that offers stunning sea views and a variety of dining and entertainment options. For those looking for a more cultural experience, the Varna Opera House and the Summer Theater offer a range of performances throughout the year.

FINAL THOUGHTS

Varna is a must-visit destination for anyone traveling to Bulgaria. With its unique mix of history, nature, and entertainment, there's something for everyone in this vibrant seaside city.

LEEUWARDEN, NETHERLANDS

Located in the northern part of the Netherlands, Leeuwarden is the capital city of the province of Friesland. With a population of around 100,000, Leeuwarden is a small but charming city that is well worth a visit for those interested in history, culture, and the arts. In this article, we will explore the various attractions and activities that make Leeuwarden a must-visit destination.

HISTORY AND ARCHITECTURE

Leeuwarden has a rich history that dates back to the 8th century. The city has been home to various rulers throughout the centuries, including the Frisians, the Saxons, and the Spanish. This history is reflected in the city's architecture, which includes buildings from various eras and styles. The Oldehove, a leaning tower that was originally part of a church, is one of Leeuwarden's most iconic landmarks. Other notable buildings include the City Hall, the Fries Museum, and the Waag, which was once a weigh house but now houses a restaurant and a museum.

CULTURE AND THE ARTS

Leeuwarden is known for its vibrant cultural scene, which includes music, theater, and art. The city hosts various cultural events throughout the year, such as the annual Frisian Horse Day, the European Capital of Culture 2018, and the Art Connection Festival. The Fries Museum is a must-visit destination for art lovers, as it houses an impressive collection of Frisian art and artifacts.

OUTDOOR ACTIVITIES

Despite its small size, Leeuwarden offers various outdoor activities for visitors to enjoy. The city is surrounded by the Frisian countryside, which is ideal for cycling and hiking. The De Alde Feanen National Park is also nearby, which is a wetland area that is home to various bird species.

CONCLUSION

In conclusion, Leeuwarden is a charming city that is rich in history, culture, and the arts. Its small size makes it easy to explore on foot or by bike, and its various attractions and activities make it a must-visit destination in the Netherlands. Whether you're interested in history, art, or outdoor activities, there's something for everyone in Leeuwarden.

BRNO, CZECH REPUBLIC

Brno, the second largest city in the Czech Republic, is often overlooked by tourists in favor of Prague. However, this vibrant city, located in the southeastern part of the country, has much to offer visitors seeking an authentic Czech experience. Here are some reasons why you should consider adding Brno to your travel itinerary.

HISTORY AND CULTURE

Brno has a rich history dating back to the 11th century, and this is evident in the city's architecture and landmarks. The Špilberk Castle, which dates back to the 13th century, is one of the most popular tourist attractions in the city. Visitors can explore the castle's history, visit the castle's museum, and enjoy panoramic views of the city from the castle's tower.

Another must-visit attraction is the Cathedral of St. Peter and Paul, which dominates the city skyline. This stunning cathedral was built in the 14th century and boasts impressive Gothic architecture. Visitors can admire the intricate details of the cathedral's interior and climb the cathedral's tower for stunning views of the city.

FOOD AND DRINK

Brno is famous for its food and drink scene, and no visit to the city is complete without sampling some of the local delicacies. Visitors can indulge in traditional Czech dishes such as svíčková, a beef sirloin served with dumplings and a creamy vegetable sauce, or knedlíky, a type of dumpling served with meat and gravy.

In addition to its food, Brno is also home to a thriving wine culture. The city is surrounded by vineyards, and visitors can enjoy wine tastings at local wineries or sample local wines at one of the city's many wine bars.

ENTERTAINMENT

Brno is a lively city with a vibrant entertainment scene. The city is home to several theaters, including the Mahen Theatre, which is one of the oldest theaters in the country. Visitors can catch a play or opera at the theater, which is known for its exceptional acoustics.

For those who prefer something more modern, Brno also has a thriving music scene. The city hosts several music festivals throughout the year, including the Brno Music Marathon, which features over 300 musicians playing across 20 venues in the city.

CONCLUSION

In conclusion, Brno is a city that offers something for everyone. With its rich history, delicious food and drink, and lively entertainment scene, Brno is a hidden gem in the heart of the Czech Republic. So why not add Brno to your travel itinerary and discover the charm of this unique and vibrant city for yourself?

GENOA, ITALY

Located in the Liguria region of northern Italy, Genoa City is often overlooked by travelers in favor of more popular destinations like Rome, Florence, and Venice. However, this port city has a rich history, beautiful architecture, and delicious cuisine that make it a must-visit destination for anyone traveling to Italy.

GETTING TO GENOA CITY

The easiest way to reach Genoa City is by flying into Genoa Cristoforo Colombo Airport, which is just a short taxi ride from the city center. Alternatively, you can take a train from major cities like Milan, Turin, or Florence.

EXPLORING THE OLD CITY

Genoa City's historic center, known as the "Old City," is a UNESCO World Heritage Site and a treasure trove of historic buildings and charming alleyways. Be sure to visit the Cattedrale di San Lorenzo, a beautiful 12th-century cathedral, and the Palazzo Ducale, a grand palace that once served as the residence of the Doge of Genoa.

DISCOVERING GENOESE CUISINE

Genoa City is famous for its cuisine, especially its seafood. Be sure to try the local specialty, pesto alla genovese, a delicious sauce made with basil, garlic, pine nuts, and Parmesan cheese. Other must-try dishes include trofie al pesto (fresh pasta with pesto sauce), focaccia di Recco (a thin, crispy flatbread filled with cheese), and farinata (a savory chickpea pancake).

EXPLORING THE PORT

As a port city, Genoa City has a long maritime history. Visit the Porto Antico (Old Port) to see historic ships and yachts and enjoy a stroll along the waterfront. Be sure to visit the Aquarium of Genoa, one of the largest aquariums in Europe, which has a wide variety of marine life from all over the world.

CONCLUSION

Genoa City may not be as well-known as some of Italy's other cities, but it has plenty to offer visitors who are looking for a more off-the-beaten-path experience. From its historic center to its delicious cuisine and beautiful port, Genoa City is a hidden gem that is well worth a visit.

ELCHE, SPAIN

Located in the province of Alicante, Elche is a historic city in Spain that is famous for its palm groves and traditional footwear industry. It is a popular tourist destination for those looking to explore the rich cultural heritage and natural beauty of the region. Here is everything you need to know about Elche.

GETTING THERE AND AROUND

Elche is well connected by air, road, and rail. Alicante-Elche Airport is the closest international airport, located about 20 kilometers away from the city center. From there, you can take a taxi, bus, or rent a car to reach Elche. The city is also accessible by train and bus from other parts of Spain. Once you're in Elche, it's easy to get around on foot, by bike, or by bus.

THE PALM GROVES

Elche is home to over 200,000 palm trees, making it one of the largest palm groves in Europe. The Palm Grove, also known as the Palmeral of Elche, has been declared a UNESCO World Heritage Site and is a must-visit attraction. The groves are dotted with parks, gardens, and museums, and you can take a guided tour to learn more about the history and significance of the palm trees.

THE HISTORIC CITY CENTER

The historic center of Elche is a charming mix of narrow streets, old buildings, and lively squares. The Basilica of Santa Maria, located in the heart of the city, is a stunning example of Gothic architecture and houses a valuable collection of art and artifacts. The Municipal Park, located near the city center, is a popular spot for locals and tourists alike, with its fountains, sculptures, and children's play areas.

THE FOOTWEAR INDUSTRY

Elche has been known for its footwear industry for centuries, and it remains a significant part of the city's economy. The Museum of Footwear, located in a 19th-century factory building, showcases the history and evolution of shoe-making in Elche, from traditional espadrilles to modern designer footwear.

FINAL THOUGHTS

Elche is a city that offers a unique blend of history, culture, and natural beauty. Whether you're interested in exploring the palm groves, admiring the architecture, or learning about the local industry, Elche has something to offer for everyone. It's a great destination for a day trip or a weekend getaway, and you're sure to leave with memories that will last a lifetime.

NEWCASTLE UPON TYNE, ENGLAND

Newcastle upon Tyne, commonly known as Newcastle, is a city located in the northeast region of England. It is a city steeped in rich history, culture, and is also known for its lively nightlife and warm hospitality.

HISTORY AND LANDMARKS

Newcastle has a fascinating history that dates back to Roman times. The city's name is derived from a castle that was built by Robert Curthose, son of William the Conqueror in 1080. The castle is still standing and is a popular tourist attraction.

Newcastle is also home to several other historical landmarks, such as the Tyne Bridge, the Angel of the North, and the Victoria Tunnel, which was originally built in the 19th century as a wagonway to transport coal from the mines to the river.

CULTURE AND ARTS

Newcastle has a vibrant cultural scene with several museums, art galleries, and theaters. The Discovery Museum, the Great North Museum, and the Laing Art Gallery are some of the popular museums and art galleries that showcase the city's rich history and culture.

The city is also home to several theaters that host a wide range of performances, from classical plays to contemporary dramas. The Theatre Royal, the Tyne Theatre and Opera House, and the Live Theatre are some of the famous theaters in Newcastle.

NIGHTLIFE AND HOSPITALITY

Newcastle is known for its lively nightlife and warm hospitality. The city has a thriving bar and club scene that caters to people of all ages and interests. From trendy bars to traditional pubs, Newcastle has something for everyone.

The city is also known for its warm hospitality, and visitors to Newcastle are sure to feel welcome. The locals are friendly and are always willing to help visitors with information and advice.

CONCLUSION

In conclusion, Newcastle upon Tyne is a vibrant city with a rich history, culture, and a lively nightlife. It is a city that has something to offer everyone, from history buffs to party animals. So if you're planning a trip to England, make sure to include Newcastle on your list of places to visit.

PULA, CROATIA

Located on the southwestern coast of the Istrian peninsula in Croatia, Pula is a historic city with a rich cultural heritage and stunning natural beauty. The city boasts an incredible mix of Roman ruins, medieval architecture, and modern amenities, making it a must-visit destination for travelers looking for an authentic Croatian experience.

HISTORY AND CULTURE

Pula's history dates back to ancient times, with evidence of human settlement dating back to the Bronze Age. The city was then inhabited by the Romans, who left behind impressive architectural marvels such as the Pula Arena, a well-preserved Roman amphitheater that can seat over 20,000 spectators. The city also features other ancient landmarks such as the Temple of Augustus, the Arch of the Sergii, and the Forum, all of which provide a glimpse into Pula's rich cultural heritage.

NATURAL BEAUTY

Pula's stunning natural beauty is equally impressive. The city is surrounded by crystal-clear waters, rugged coastlines, and verdant forests, making it an ideal destination for outdoor enthusiasts. Visitors can enjoy hiking, cycling, and kayaking in the nearby nature reserves or simply relax on one of the many pristine beaches.

FOOD AND DRINK

Pula is also known for its delicious cuisine and wine. The city's proximity to the sea means that seafood is a staple on many menus, with dishes such as grilled fish and octopus salad being popular choices. Additionally, the region is famous for its wine, with numerous vineyards and wineries producing high-quality wines that are sure to impress even the most discerning wine lover.

ACCOMMODATION

Pula offers a wide range of accommodation options to suit all budgets, from luxury hotels to affordable guesthouses and apartments. Many of the hotels are located in the city center, providing easy access to the main attractions, while others are situated in more secluded areas for those seeking peace and quiet.

CONCLUSION

In conclusion, Pula is a city that offers a unique blend of history, culture, natural beauty, and modern amenities. Whether you're looking to explore ancient ruins, soak up the sun on a pristine beach, or indulge in delicious food and wine, Pula has something to offer everyone. So why not add this stunning city to your travel itinerary and discover all that it has to offer?

TAMPERE, FINLAND

Tampere, located in the southern part of Finland, is a city that has a lot to offer to tourists. It is the third-largest city in Finland, and it is known for its rich culture, vibrant nightlife, and beautiful scenery. In this article, we will explore some of the top attractions that you should visit when you're in Tampere.

CULTURE

Tampere is known for its cultural diversity and rich history. The city is home to numerous museums and art galleries that showcase the region's history and art. The Tampere Art Museum, for instance, houses over 6,000 pieces of art, including works by Finnish artists such as Akseli Gallen-Kallela and Eero Järnefelt. You can also visit the Tampereen Teatteri, the city's premier theater, which features plays, musicals, and other cultural events.

NATURAL BEAUTY

Tampere is surrounded by beautiful lakes and forests, making it a great destination for nature lovers. Pyynikki Observation Tower offers a panoramic view of the city and is situated in a lush forest. You can also explore the Näsinneula Observation Tower, which is the tallest observation tower in the Nordic countries. The tower offers a breathtaking view of the surrounding lake and forest.

CULINARY DELIGHTS

Tampere has a thriving food scene that caters to different tastes and preferences. The city's food culture is heavily influenced by its location and history. Tampere's must-try dish is the black sausage, also known as 'mustamakkara,' which is made of pork, blood, and barley. You can find it in the Tammelantori market, where it is served with lingonberry jam and a cup of coffee.

NIGHTLIFE

Tampere's nightlife is vibrant and diverse, with something for everyone. The city has a wide variety of bars and clubs that cater to different tastes and preferences. If you're looking for a lively and energetic atmosphere, head to Plevna, the city's largest brewery and restaurant complex. It offers a variety of beers and ales that are brewed on-site.

IN CONCLUSION

Tampere is a city that has something to offer for everyone. Whether you're interested in exploring the city's culture, natural beauty, food scene, or nightlife, Tampere has it all. So, next time you're planning a trip to Finland, make sure to add Tampere to your itinerary.

HELSINGBORG, SWEDEN

Helsingborg is a picturesque coastal city in the southern part of Sweden, overlooking the Öresund Strait that separates Sweden from Denmark. The city boasts a rich history, stunning architecture, and a vibrant cultural scene that attracts tourists from all over the world.

GETTING TO HELSINGBORG

Helsingborg is easily accessible by train, bus, and car. The city has a well-connected train station that links it to major cities in Sweden, Denmark, and other neighboring countries. The nearest international airport is the Copenhagen Airport, located just 30 minutes away from Helsingborg by train.

EXPLORING THE CITY

Helsingborg is a small city that can be easily explored on foot or by bike. The city center is packed with quaint cafes, boutique shops, and historic buildings that reflect the city's rich cultural heritage. One of the most popular attractions in Helsingborg is the medieval castle, Kärnan, which dates back to the 14th century and offers stunning views of the city and the strait.

For a taste of Helsingborg's maritime history, visitors can visit the Dunkers Cultural Centre, which showcases the city's seafaring traditions through interactive exhibits and displays. The city also has several museums, such as the Helsingborg City Museum and the Fredriksdal Open-Air Museum, which offer fascinating insights into the city's past and present.

FOOD AND DRINK

Helsingborg has a thriving food and drink scene, with a wide variety of restaurants, cafes, and bars to suit all tastes and budgets. The city is particularly famous for its seafood, which is served fresh and delicious in many of the local restaurants. Visitors can also sample traditional Swedish delicacies, such as meatballs, lingonberry jam, and cinnamon buns, in the city's bakeries and cafes.

SHOPPING

Helsingborg is a shopper's paradise, with a range of shops and boutiques that cater to all tastes and budgets. The city center is home to many independent stores selling unique and handmade items, as well as high-end fashion boutiques and popular chain stores.

CONCLUSION

Helsingborg is a hidden gem that offers a perfect blend of history, culture, and natural beauty. Whether you're looking to explore the city's rich heritage, relax on its beautiful beaches, or enjoy its vibrant food and drink scene, Helsingborg is sure to delight and enchant visitors of all ages and interests.

BATH, ENGLAND

Bath City, located in the southwestern part of England, is a popular tourist destination known for its rich history, stunning architecture, and natural hot springs. This charming city is perfect for travelers who want to immerse themselves in the beauty of English culture, as well as experience the luxurious relaxation of the city's famous spa facilities.

HISTORY AND CULTURE

Bath City has a rich history that dates back to the Roman times, when the city was known for its hot springs and was named Aquae Sulis. The city's Roman Baths, which have been preserved to this day, are a must-visit attraction for history buffs. Visitors can also explore the impressive Georgian architecture, including the iconic Royal Crescent and Circus, which are both examples of the city's unique architectural style.

HOT SPRINGS AND SPA TREATMENTS

One of the main draws of Bath City is its natural hot springs, which have been used for relaxation and healing for thousands of years. Visitors can soak in the warm, mineral-rich waters at the Thermae Bath Spa, a modern spa facility that offers a range of treatments and experiences. The spa's rooftop pool also provides a breathtaking view of the city and its surroundings.

ARTS AND CULTURE SCENE

Bath City has a vibrant arts and culture scene, with numerous museums, galleries, and theaters to explore. The city's largest museum, the Victoria Art Gallery, houses an impressive collection of British art, including works by Thomas Gainsborough and Walter Sickert. The city is also home to the Theatre Royal, a historic venue that has hosted productions since the late 18th century.

SHOPPING AND DINING

Bath City offers a range of shopping and dining options, from trendy boutiques and artisanal shops to traditional English pubs and fine dining restaurants. Visitors can browse the eclectic mix of independent stores in the city center or visit the bustling weekly markets for locally sourced produce and crafts. Foodies will enjoy the city's diverse culinary scene, which includes everything from traditional English fare to international cuisine.

CONCLUSION

Bath City is a must-visit destination for travelers who want to experience the rich history, culture, and natural beauty of England. With its stunning architecture, natural hot springs, vibrant arts scene, and diverse dining options, this charming city has something to offer everyone. So why not book your trip today and discover the magic of Bath City for yourself?

ESKISEHIR, TURKEY

When people think of Turkey, the first cities that come to mind are Istanbul, Ankara, and Izmir. However, Eskişehir is a hidden gem that is worth exploring for its unique culture, beautiful landscapes, and historical landmarks.

GETTING TO ESKISEHIR

Eskisehir has a well-developed transportation system, including buses, trains, and flights. The city is located approximately 230 kilometers away from Istanbul, and you can take a direct flight to Eskisehir from Istanbul's Sabiha Gökçen International Airport. Alternatively, you can take a bus or train from Istanbul or any other major city in Turkey.

LOCATION AND HISTORY

Located in the northwest of Central Anatolia, Eskişehir has a rich history that dates back to the Phrygian era. It was later ruled by the Lydians, Persians, and Macedonians before becoming part of the Ottoman Empire in the 14th century. The city was a major industrial hub during the Ottoman era and became an important center for education and culture after the Republic of Turkey was established in 1923.

CULTURE AND ART

Eskişehir is known for its vibrant cultural scene and artistic atmosphere. The city hosts several cultural festivals throughout the year, such as the International Eskisehir Film Festival and the International Meerschaum Festival. The Meerschaum Museum and the Contemporary Glass Art Museum are also worth visiting to explore the city's artistic heritage.

LANDMARKS AND NATURAL ATTRACTIONS

The city is home to several historical landmarks, including the Ottoman-style Odunpazarı district, the Kurşunlu Mosque, and the Sivrihisar Castle. The Archaeological Museum of Eskişehir showcases the city's ancient history and artifacts from different periods. The Porsuk River, which runs through the city, is a popular spot for boat tours and picnics.

FOOD AND CUISINE

Eskişehir's cuisine is a blend of Ottoman and Anatolian flavors. The city's famous dishes include çibörek, a pastry filled with spiced minced meat, and yaprak sarma, stuffed grape leaves. Other must-try dishes are etli ekmek, a Turkish-style pizza, and keşkek, a traditional dish made with meat and wheat.

CONCLUSION

Eskişehir is a charming city that offers a unique blend of culture, history, and natural beauty. It is a perfect destination for those looking to escape the hustle and bustle of big cities and explore the lesser-known parts of Turkey. So, the next time you plan a trip to Turkey, make sure to add Eskişehir to your itinerary.

LAUSANNE, SWITZERLAND

Lausanne is a beautiful city located in the French-speaking part of Switzerland, situated on the shores of Lake Geneva. It is the capital of the canton of Vaud and is known for its rich history, beautiful architecture, and breathtaking scenery. With so much to explore and discover, Lausanne is a perfect destination for travelers who want to experience the best of Switzerland.

GETTING TO LAUSANNE

Lausanne is easily accessible by train, bus, and car. The city is just 40 minutes away from Geneva by train and 2 hours from Zurich. Visitors can also take a scenic boat ride across Lake Geneva to reach Lausanne.

EXPLORING THE CITY

Lausanne is a compact city, and most of the major attractions are within walking distance of each other. The Old Town of Lausanne is a must-visit destination for travelers. It is home to the stunning Gothic-style Lausanne Cathedral, which offers stunning panoramic views of the city and the lake.

Visitors can also explore the charming streets of the Old Town, which are lined with historic buildings, shops, and restaurants. The Place de la Palud is a popular square in the Old Town, known for its beautiful fountain and the impressive medieval clock tower.

Lausanne is also home to several museums, including the Olympic Museum, which showcases the history of the Olympic Games. The Musée de l'Elysée is a must-visit destination for photography lovers, while the Musée de la Boverie features a diverse collection of art from around the world.

ENJOYING THE OUTDOORS

Lausanne is surrounded by beautiful natural landscapes and is a perfect destination for outdoor enthusiasts. The Lavaux Vineyard Terraces, a UNESCO World Heritage Site, is located just outside the city and is known for its beautiful vineyards and stunning views of Lake Geneva.

Visitors can also take a stroll along the scenic Ouchy Promenade, which offers stunning views of the lake and the Alps. The Parc de la Grange is another popular destination, known for its beautiful gardens and fountains.

GETTING AROUND LAUSANNE

Lausanne has an excellent public transportation system, including buses, trains, and a metro. The Lausanne Transport Card is a free transportation pass provided to all visitors staying in Lausanne hotels, which allows them to travel around the city for free.

CONCLUSION

Lausanne is a beautiful city that offers something for everyone. With its rich history, beautiful architecture, and stunning natural landscapes, Lausanne is a perfect destination for travelers who want to experience the best of Switzerland. Whether you are interested in exploring the city's history, enjoying the outdoors, or simply relaxing by the lake, Lausanne is a must-visit destination.

SIBIU, ROMANIA

Sibiu is a city located in the heart of Transylvania, Romania. The city is known for its rich history, vibrant culture, and stunning architecture. It's a destination that's perfect for travelers looking for a unique and authentic experience.

A WALK-THROUGH HISTORY

Sibiu has a fascinating history that can be traced back to the 12th century. The city was once a major center of commerce and trade, and it has been shaped by the many cultures and civilizations that have called it home. Walking through Sibiu's streets is like taking a trip back in time. Visitors can admire the Gothic architecture of the Evangelical Church, the Renaissance-style Brukenthal Palace, and the Baroque-style Orthodox Cathedral.

CULTURE AND FESTIVALS

Sibiu is also known for its vibrant cultural scene. The city is home to numerous museums and galleries, showcasing the works of some of Romania's most talented artists. The city's theater scene is also very active, with regular performances taking place at the State Theater and the Radu Stanca National Theater. Sibiu is also famous for its many festivals and events, including the International Theater Festival, the Sibiu Jazz Festival, and the Transylvania International Film Festival.

EXPLORING THE OUTDOORS

For nature lovers, Sibiu offers plenty of opportunities to explore the great outdoors. Visitors can take a stroll through the beautiful Sub Arini Park or hike through the nearby Făgăraș Mountains. The Transfagarasan Road, one of the most scenic drives in the world, is also located near Sibiu.

GETTING AROUND

Getting around Sibiu is easy, thanks to its well-connected public transportation system. The city is also very pedestrian-friendly, with many attractions located within walking distance of each other.

IN CONCLUSION

Sibiu is a city that has something for everyone. From its rich history and stunning architecture to its vibrant cultural scene and beautiful natural landscapes, it's a destination that's sure to leave a lasting impression on any traveler.

LÜBECK, GERMANY

If you're looking to explore a lesser-known city in Germany, Lübeck is the perfect destination. This charming town, located in the northern state of Schleswig-Holstein, has a rich history and beautiful architecture that will transport you back in time.

HISTORY AND ARCHITECTURE

Lübeck is known as the "Queen of the Hanseatic League," a medieval trading alliance that dominated Northern Europe during the 14th and 15th centuries. As a result, the city has a rich cultural heritage, evident in its stunning architecture. The Old Town of Lübeck, which is a UNESCO World Heritage Site, is a testament to the city's prosperous past. The city boasts an impressive collection of Gothic-style buildings, including the Holstentor Gate, St. Mary's Church, and the Town Hall. The charming cobblestone streets and narrow alleys add to the city's old-world charm.

CULTURE AND CUISINE

Lübeck is also known for its marzipan, a sweet almond-based confectionary that originated in the city in the 15th century. You can sample the local specialty at Café Niederegger, a café and shop that has been producing marzipan since 1806. Additionally, Lübeck hosts several cultural events throughout the year, including the Lübeck Christmas Market, which takes place in the historic market square and is one of the most popular Christmas markets in Northern Germany.

ACTIVITIES AND ATTRACTIONS

There are plenty of things to do in Lübeck, whether you're interested in history, art, or simply wandering around the city's picturesque streets. The St. Anne's Museum Quarter is home to several museums, including the Museum of Art and Cultural History and the Museum of Nature and the Environment. The Buddenbrook House, the former home of Nobel Prize-winning author Thomas Mann, is also located in Lübeck and is open to visitors. For a panoramic view of the city, climb the tower of St. Peter's Church, the tallest church in Lübeck.

CONCLUSION

Lübeck may not be as well-known as other German cities like Berlin or Munich, but it's definitely worth a visit. With its rich history, stunning architecture, delicious cuisine, and cultural events, Lübeck has something to offer everyone. So, if you're planning a trip to Germany, be sure to add Lübeck to your itinerary.

PALERMO, ITALY

Palermo is the vibrant and bustling capital of Sicily, an island region of Italy located in the Mediterranean Sea. With a history dating back more than 2,700 years, the city is a melting pot of different cultures, reflected in its architecture, cuisine, and traditions.

GETTING TO PALERMO

Palermo has an international airport, Falcone-Borsellino Airport, which serves direct flights from major European cities. You can also reach Palermo by ferry from Naples, Genoa, and other Italian ports. Once you arrive, the best way to get around the city is on foot or by public transportation.

SIGHTS AND ATTRACTIONS

Palermo is a city that rewards wandering and exploration. Its historic center, known as the Quattro Canti, is a beautiful example of Baroque architecture. The Norman Palace and the Cathedral of Palermo are must-sees, as well as the Teatro Massimo, one of the largest opera houses in Europe. The Vucciria Market is a sensory overload of sights and smells, with vendors selling fresh produce, seafood, and traditional Sicilian street food.

FOOD AND DRINK

Sicilian cuisine is renowned for its seafood, citrus fruits, and sweet pastries. Palermo is no exception, with a vibrant street food scene and a wealth of traditional restaurants. Arancine, deep-fried rice balls stuffed with meat or cheese, are a local specialty, as well as cannoli, sweet pastries filled with ricotta cheese. Don't miss the opportunity to try Palermo's signature dish, pasta con le sarde, a pasta dish made with sardines, fennel, pine nuts, and raisins.

CULTURE AND TRADITIONS

Palermo is a city with a strong sense of tradition, from its colorful festivals to its vibrant street life. The Feast of Santa Rosalia, held in July, is one of the city's biggest celebrations, with processions, fireworks, and street parties. The Palermo International Jazz Festival, held in October, attracts musicians and jazz lovers from around the world. Palermo is also home to some of Italy's most famous puppet theaters, which stage traditional Sicilian puppet shows.

ACCOMMODATION

Palermo has a range of accommodation options, from luxury hotels to budget-friendly hostels. Many visitors choose to stay in the historic center, where they can easily explore the city's sights and attractions on foot. Other popular areas include the seafront neighborhood of Mondello, which has a beautiful beach, and the upscale neighborhood of Politeama, which is known for its shopping and nightlife.

CONCLUSION

Palermo is a city that rewards those who are willing to explore and immerse themselves in its rich culture and history. Whether you're interested in art and architecture, food and drink, or music and festivals, Palermo has something to offer. With its warm climate, stunning coastline, and vibrant street life, it's no wonder that Palermo is known as Sicily's cultural capital.

YORK, ENGLAND

Located in the north of England, York is a city steeped in history, boasting a rich heritage that dates back to the Roman era. This charming city is a popular tourist destination and for good reason - it has something to offer for everyone, from ancient Roman walls to stunning Gothic cathedrals and a thriving food and drink scene.

GETTING TO YORK

York is easily accessible by train from major cities such as London and Edinburgh, with a journey time of approximately two hours from either city. If you prefer driving, York is well connected to the national motorway network, with the M1, M62, and A1(M) all passing close by.

HISTORICAL ATTRACTIONS

York is a city that is rich in history, and there are many fascinating historical attractions to explore. The most famous of these is the York Minster, a stunning Gothic cathedral that dates back to the 7th century. The cathedral is one of the largest of its kind in northern Europe and is an absolute must-visit for anyone interested in history and architecture. Another popular attraction is the York Castle Museum, which is housed in a former prison and gives visitors a glimpse into what life was like in the past.

FOOD AND DRINK

York is also known for its thriving food and drink scene, with an array of excellent restaurants, pubs, and cafes to choose from. For a quintessential Yorkshire experience, head to Betty's Tea Rooms for a cup of tea and a slice of cake. Alternatively, sample some local delicacies such as Yorkshire pudding or Parkin cake.

SHOPPING

York is a great destination for shoppers, with a mix of independent boutiques and well-known high street brands. The Shambles is a narrow medieval street that is home to many unique shops and is a must-visit for anyone who loves shopping.

CONCLUSION

York is a city that is steeped in history and has something to offer for everyone. Whether you're interested in exploring ancient Roman walls or sampling some of the local delicacies, you're sure to have a great time in this charming city. So why not plan a visit to York today and discover everything this historic and cultural gem of the north has to offer?

MONS, BELGIUM

Nestled in the heart of Wallonia, Belgium, Mons city is a charming destination for those seeking a taste of traditional Belgian culture. With its rich history, stunning architecture, and delicious cuisine, Mons has something for everyone. In this article, we will explore the best of what Mons city has to offer.

HISTORY AND CULTURE

Mons city has a fascinating history that dates back to the Neolithic period. The city was under Roman rule for several centuries, and its strategic location made it a coveted prize for many invading armies throughout the ages. Today, Mons is known for its beautiful historic buildings, including the UNESCO World Heritage site, the Belfry of Mons.

One of the city's most significant cultural events is the Doudou Festival, which takes place annually on Trinity Sunday. This festival commemorates the legendary battle between Saint George and the Dragon, and it features a variety of traditional activities, such as processions, music, and dancing.

ARCHITECTURE AND LANDMARKS

Mons city is home to a plethora of stunning architectural marvels, ranging from Gothic and Baroque to Art Nouveau and contemporary styles. The Grand Place, the city's central square, is a prime example of Mons' rich architectural heritage, with its ornate buildings, fountains, and cobblestone streets.

Another must-visit landmark in Mons is the Mundaneum, a unique museum that celebrates the history of human knowledge. This museum is home to a vast collection of books, photographs, and documents that tell the story of human progress over the centuries.

CUISINE

Belgian cuisine is renowned worldwide for its delicious waffles, chocolates, and beer, and Mons is no exception. The city is home to a variety of excellent restaurants and cafes, serving up a range of traditional Belgian dishes, such as moules-frites (mussels and fries) and carbonnade flamande (beef stew).

For those with a sweet tooth, Mons is the perfect destination, with its many chocolatiers and patisseries offering a wide range of mouth-watering treats, from pralines to macarons.

FINAL THOUGHTS

Mons city is a hidden gem of Wallonia, offering visitors a taste of traditional Belgian culture and history. Whether you're interested in architecture, cuisine, or cultural events, Mons has something for everyone. So why not plan a visit to Mons city and discover its many delights for yourself?

DUNDEE, SCOTLAND

Dundee is a vibrant city situated in the east of Scotland, known for its rich history, beautiful architecture, and stunning scenery. Whether you're a history buff, an art lover, or an outdoor enthusiast, Dundee has something for everyone.

CULTURE AND ART

Dundee has a rich cultural heritage, and the city boasts a thriving arts scene. The Dundee Contemporary Arts (DCA) is a fantastic venue that showcases a diverse range of contemporary art exhibitions, films, and events. The McManus Galleries is another must-visit attraction, displaying a vast collection of art, artifacts, and natural history exhibits.

HISTORY AND ARCHITECTURE

If you're interested in history and architecture, Dundee has a lot to offer. The city is home to numerous historic landmarks, including the Dundee Law, a 174-meter-high hill that offers panoramic views of the city and the River Tay. Another iconic landmark is the Dundee Rep Theatre, a beautifully restored 1930s Art Deco building that hosts an array of performances and events throughout the year.

OUTDOOR ADVENTURES

Dundee's natural beauty and scenery offer endless opportunities for outdoor adventures. The city is surrounded by rolling hills, lush forests, and stunning coastlines, making it the perfect destination for hiking, cycling, and water sports. The city's two parks, Camperdown Country Park and Lochee Park, are perfect for picnics, strolls, and family outings.

FOOD AND DRINK

Dundee is also home to a vibrant food and drink scene, with plenty of restaurants, cafes, and bars to suit all tastes and budgets. The city is famous for its traditional Scottish cuisine, such as haggis, neeps, and tatties, as well as its delicious seafood, including fresh fish and shellfish caught in the nearby waters.

FINAL THOUGHTS

Dundee is a city full of surprises, and there's always something new to discover. From its rich cultural heritage to its stunning natural beauty, the city has something for everyone. Whether you're exploring the city's historic landmarks, indulging in its delicious food and drink scene, or embarking on outdoor adventures, Dundee is a destination that won't disappoint.

SOPOT, POLAND

Located on the Baltic coast of Poland, Sopot is a beautiful and charming city that is worth visiting. Known for its stunning beaches, lively nightlife, and rich history, Sopot has something to offer for everyone.

GETTING THERE

Sopot is easily accessible by train from major cities like Warsaw and Gdansk. Alternatively, it is just a short drive from Gdansk Lech Walesa Airport, which offers direct flights from various European cities.

EXPLORING THE CITY

The highlight of Sopot is its beautiful beach, which stretches for miles along the coast. Visitors can enjoy swimming in the crystal-clear waters, soaking up the sun, and taking a stroll along the promenade. There are also plenty of bars, restaurants, and cafes in the area, where you can indulge in delicious Polish cuisine.

Apart from the beach, Sopot is also home to several historic landmarks. The Sopot Pier, which is one of the longest wooden piers in Europe, offers a stunning view of the city's coastline. The Crooked House, a unique building that resembles a distorted fairytale house, is another popular tourist attraction.

NIGHTLIFE IN SOPOT

Sopot is known for its vibrant nightlife, with plenty of bars, clubs, and casinos to choose from. The city is especially lively during the summer months, when tourists flock to the beaches and the clubs stay open until dawn.

ACCOMMODATIONS IN SOPOT

There are plenty of accommodation options in Sopot, ranging from budget-friendly hostels to luxury hotels. Visitors can choose to stay in the city center or opt for a beachfront property with stunning views of the sea.

IN CONCLUSION

Sopot is a hidden gem on the Polish coast that is definitely worth a visit. With its stunning beaches, rich history, and vibrant nightlife, there is something for everyone in this charming city. So pack your bags and head to Sopot for an unforgettable vacation!

BURSA, TURKEY

Located in the northwestern region of Turkey, Bursa City is a hidden gem that offers a unique blend of history, culture, and natural beauty. Known as the "Green City," Bursa boasts stunning mountain views, lush gardens, and parks that make it a great destination for nature lovers. With its rich history and ancient landmarks, the city also appeals to those interested in Turkish history and architecture.

GETTING TO BURSA

The easiest way to get to Bursa is by flying into Istanbul and then taking a ferry or bus to the city. The ferry ride takes about 1.5 hours, while the bus ride takes around 3 hours. Alternatively, you can also take a direct flight to Bursa Yenisehir Airport, which is located about 45 minutes from the city center.

HISTORICAL LANDMARKS

Bursa is home to many historical landmarks, including the Great Mosque, the Green Mosque, and the Green Tomb. The Great Mosque, also known as the Ulu Camii, is one of the largest and oldest mosques in Turkey, dating back to the 14th century. The Green Mosque, named for its beautiful green tiles, was built in the 15th century and is a stunning example of Ottoman architecture. The Green Tomb, located adjacent to the Green Mosque, is the final resting place of Sultan Mehmet I and is decorated with intricate tilework and calligraphy.

NATURAL BEAUTY

Bursa's natural beauty is a major draw for tourists. The city is surrounded by the Uludag National Park, which offers hiking, skiing, and camping opportunities. The park is home to diverse flora and fauna, including bears, wolves, and lynxes. The city also boasts many beautiful parks and gardens, such as the Emir Sultan Park and the Bursa Botanical Park, which are great spots for a relaxing stroll or picnic.

CUISINE

No visit to Bursa is complete without trying its famous cuisine. The city is known for its delicious Iskender kebab, a dish made with thinly sliced lamb, tomato sauce, and melted butter. Another local specialty is the candied chestnuts, which are sold on the streets and make for a sweet and tasty snack.

CONCLUSION

Bursa City is a must-visit destination for anyone traveling to Turkey. With its historical landmarks, natural beauty, and delicious cuisine, there is something for everyone to enjoy. Don't miss out on the chance to discover this hidden gem and experience the charms of the "Green City" for yourself.

HUELVA, SPAIN

Huelva is a city located in the Andalusian region of southern Spain, and while it may not be as famous as other Spanish cities such as Barcelona or Madrid, it is definitely a hidden gem worth exploring. Here's a quick guide to the city.

LOCATION AND HISTORY

Huelva is located on the western coast of Spain, just a short distance from the border with Portugal. The city has a rich history that dates back to the Roman era, and it was an important port during the colonial period when Spain was exploring and colonizing the New World.

THINGS TO SEE AND DO

Huelva may be a small city, but there are plenty of things to see and do here. The city is home to a number of museums, including the Museum of Huelva, which showcases the history and culture of the city and its surrounding area. The city also has a number of historic buildings and monuments, including the Cathedral of Huelva, which dates back to the 17th century.

Nature lovers will appreciate the nearby natural parks, such as the Doñana National Park, which is a UNESCO World Heritage site and one of the largest nature reserves in Europe. The park is home to a variety of wildlife, including the endangered Iberian lynx.

FOOD AND DRINK

Huelva is known for its seafood, and there are plenty of restaurants in the city where you can try fresh seafood dishes. The city is also home to a number of wineries, where you can taste the local wines and learn about the winemaking process.

BEACHES

The city is also known for its beaches, such as the Playa de la Bota, which is located just outside the city center. The beach is known for its crystal-clear water and fine sand.

CONCLUSION

If you're planning a trip to southern Spain, be sure to add Huelva to your itinerary. With its rich history, natural beauty, delicious food, and beautiful beaches, it's a city that is definitely worth exploring.

NIJMEGEN, NETHERLANDS

Nijmegen is a beautiful city located in the eastern part of the Netherlands. It is known for its rich history, beautiful scenery, and vibrant cultural scene. Whether you're interested in history, nature, or nightlife, there is something for everyone in Nijmegen.

HISTORY AND CULTURE

Nijmegen is one of the oldest cities in the Netherlands, with a history that dates back to Roman times. The city has a rich cultural heritage, which is reflected in its architecture, museums, and art galleries. The city is also home to a large student population, which contributes to its lively and diverse cultural scene.

One of the most famous landmarks in Nijmegen is the Waalbrug bridge, which was built in the 1930s and is considered one of the most beautiful bridges in the Netherlands. The Valkhof Museum is another must-see attraction, which showcases the city's Roman history and features an impressive collection of medieval art.

NATURE AND OUTDOORS

Nijmegen is located on the banks of the Waal river, which offers plenty of opportunities for outdoor activities such as cycling and hiking. The city is also home to a large park called the Goffertpark, which is a popular spot for picnics and concerts during the summer months.

NIGHTLIFE AND ENTERTAINMENT

Nijmegen is known for its lively nightlife scene, with plenty of bars, clubs, and restaurants to choose from. The city also hosts several festivals throughout the year, including the Four Days Marches, which is the largest walking event in the world, and the Summer Festival, which features live music and entertainment.

CONCLUSION

Nijmegen is a charming Dutch city that has something for everyone. Whether you're interested in history, nature, or nightlife, you're sure to find plenty of things to see and do in this vibrant and welcoming city. So why not plan a trip to Nijmegen today and discover all that this wonderful city has to offer?

GUIMARAES, PORTUGAL

Nestled in the north of Portugal, Guimaraes is a charming and historic city that offers a wealth of cultural and architectural wonders. It is often referred to as the "birthplace of Portugal" and is considered one of the country's most important cities.

GETTING TO GUIMARAES

Guimaraes can be easily reached by car or public transportation from Porto or Lisbon. If you are coming from Porto, you can take a direct train that will take you to Guimaraes in less than an hour.

HISTORIC CENTER

One of the highlights of visiting Guimaraes is exploring its historic center, which has been declared a UNESCO World Heritage Site. The narrow streets and picturesque houses transport you back in time, and you can discover stunning medieval architecture and hidden squares.

THE CASTLE OF GUIMARAES

The Castle of Guimaraes is one of the most impressive landmarks in the city. This medieval fortress played an essential role in the formation of the Portuguese kingdom, and visitors can learn about the country's history while admiring the castle's stunning views.

THE DUKES OF BRAGANZA

Another must-see attraction in Guimaraes is the Palace of the Dukes of Braganza. This 15th-century palace is one of the most important examples of Portuguese architecture from that era. You can explore its grand halls and galleries and learn about the lives of the Portuguese nobility.

LOCAL CUISINE

Portuguese cuisine is renowned worldwide, and Guimaraes is no exception. Make sure to try the local specialties, such as the "caldo verde" soup, the "bacalhau" (codfish), and the "francesinha" (a sandwich with meat, cheese, and a special sauce).

NIGHTLIFE

Guimaraes' nightlife is vibrant and varied, with options for all tastes. From cozy bars to trendy nightclubs, you can find plenty of places to have a fun night out.

CONCLUSION

Guimaraes is a charming and historic city that offers a unique blend of cultural and culinary delights. Whether you are interested in history, architecture, or simply want to enjoy the Portuguese lifestyle, Guimaraes is a destination you won't want to miss.

LARNACA, CYPRUS

Located on the southeastern coast of Cyprus, Larnaca is a city known for its rich history, stunning beaches, and vibrant culture. Whether you're a history buff, a beach lover, or simply looking for a relaxing getaway, Larnaca has something to offer for everyone.

HISTORY AND CULTURE

Larnaca has a fascinating history that dates back to the Neolithic period, and the city is home to a number of historic landmarks and archaeological sites that showcase its rich past. One of the must-see attractions in Larnaca is the Hala Sultan Tekke, a mosque that is considered to be one of the holiest sites in Islam. The city also has a number of museums, such as the Larnaca District Archaeological Museum, that showcase the cultural and historical significance of the area.

BEACHES AND WATER ACTIVITIES

One of the biggest draws of Larnaca is its stunning beaches, which offer crystal-clear waters and soft, golden sands. Finikoudes Beach is the most popular beach in the city and is known for its lively atmosphere and excellent water sports facilities. Other great beaches in the area include Mackenzie Beach, a popular spot for windsurfing and kiteboarding, and CTO Beach, which is ideal for families with young children.

FOOD AND DRINK

Larnaca is a foodie's paradise, with a wide variety of restaurants and cafes that offer everything from traditional Cypriot dishes to international cuisine. The city is known for its seafood, and visitors should make sure to try the grilled octopus, fresh fish, and squid dishes. There are also plenty of local wines and beers to sample, as well as a range of delicious desserts and pastries.

NIGHTLIFE

Larnaca has a vibrant nightlife scene that caters to all tastes, from sophisticated cocktail bars to lively nightclubs. The city is particularly known for its beach bars, which offer stunning views of the Mediterranean and a relaxed atmosphere. Many of the bars and clubs are located in the Finikoudes area, making it easy to hop from one venue to another.

ACCOMMODATION

Larnaca has a range of accommodation options to suit all budgets and preferences, from luxury resorts to budget-friendly guesthouses. Many of the hotels are located along the seafront, offering stunning views of the Mediterranean and easy access to the beaches and attractions.

CONCLUSION

With its rich history, stunning beaches, vibrant culture, and delicious food, Larnaca is a must-visit destination for anyone traveling to Cyprus. Whether you're looking for a relaxing getaway or an action-packed adventure, you're sure to find something to love in this charming city.

DEBRECEN, HUNGARY

Debrecen, Hungary's second-largest city, is a hidden gem in the country's eastern region. Located just a few hours away from Budapest, this vibrant city offers a unique blend of culture, history, and natural beauty. Whether you're a history buff, a nature lover, or a foodie, Debrecen has something for everyone.

GETTING TO DEBRECEN

The easiest way to get to Debrecen is by plane. The city has its own airport, the Debrecen International Airport, which is well-connected to major cities in Europe. If you're coming from Budapest, you can take a train or bus to Debrecen, which takes around 2-3 hours.

EXPLORING THE CITY

Debrecen's historic city center is a must-visit for any traveler. The centerpiece of the city is the Great Reformed Church, which is the largest Protestant church in Hungary. The church's beautiful architecture and rich history make it a popular tourist attraction. Another must-see attraction is the Déri Museum, which houses a vast collection of art and artifacts from around the world.

Nature lovers will enjoy the city's parks and green spaces. The Nagyerdő Park is the largest park in Debrecen, and it offers a variety of activities, including hiking, biking, and picnicking. The nearby Hortobágy National Park, which is a UNESCO World Heritage site, is also worth a visit.

FOOD AND DRINK

Debrecen is known for its hearty cuisine and local specialties. One of the most popular dishes in the city is the Debreceni sausage, which is a smoked sausage made from pork. Other local specialties include goulash, stuffed cabbage, and chimney cake. To wash it all down, try a glass of pálinka, a traditional Hungarian fruit brandy.

FINAL THOUGHTS

Debrecen may not be as well-known as some of Hungary's other cities, but it's a hidden gem that's definitely worth a visit. With its rich history, stunning architecture, and natural beauty, Debrecen has something to offer everyone. Whether you're looking for a cultural experience or just a relaxing getaway, Debrecen won't disappoint.

PESCARA, ITALY

Located on the eastern coast of Italy, Pescara is a stunning city that offers an incredible mix of history, culture, and natural beauty. It is a hidden gem that often goes unnoticed by tourists, but it is definitely worth a visit. Here's everything you need to know about this charming Italian city.

GETTING THERE

Pescara is conveniently located on the Adriatic coast, which makes it easily accessible by air, train, or car. The city has its own airport, the Abruzzo Airport, which offers direct flights to many European cities. If you prefer traveling by train, Pescara has two train stations, the Pescara Centrale and Pescara Porta Nuova, that connect it to other major Italian cities.

EXPLORING THE CITY

Once you arrive in Pescara, you'll find that there's plenty to see and do. The city has a rich history, and you can explore its past by visiting the Museo Archeologico Nazionale d'Abruzzo, which houses a fascinating collection of ancient artifacts. For a taste of local culture, head to the Teatro Massimo, a beautiful theater that hosts concerts, operas, and other cultural events.

If you're a nature lover, you'll be pleased to know that Pescara is surrounded by breathtaking scenery. The city is located at the foot of the Maiella mountain range, which offers endless opportunities for hiking and other outdoor activities. The nearby beaches are also a major draw, with crystal-clear waters and soft sand perfect for sunbathing or swimming.

EATING AND DRINKING

One of the best things about visiting Italy is enjoying the delicious food and wine, and Pescara is no exception. The city has many restaurants and cafes that offer traditional Italian cuisine, as well as local specialties like seafood and olive oil. And of course, no trip to Italy is complete without sampling the local wines, such as Montepulciano d'Abruzzo and Trebbiano d'Abruzzo.

WHERE TO STAY

Pescara has a wide range of accommodation options to suit all budgets and preferences. Whether you're looking for a luxury hotel or a cozy bed and breakfast, you'll find something that meets your needs. Some of the best places to stay include the Hotel Carlton, Hotel Ambra Palace, and Hotel Victoria.

FINAL THOUGHTS

Pescara is a hidden gem that offers something for everyone. Whether you're interested in history, culture, nature, or food, you'll find plenty to enjoy in this charming Italian city. So why not add Pescara to your travel itinerary and experience all that it has to offer?

YAROSLAVL, RUSSIA

Yaroslavl city is a gem of a destination that is often overlooked by tourists. This city, located in the central part of Russia, is one of the oldest and most beautiful cities in the country. With a rich history and culture, Yaroslavl is a must-visit destination for anyone interested in exploring Russia beyond its more famous cities.

LOCATION AND HISTORY

Located on the banks of the Volga River, Yaroslavl was founded in the 11th century and served as an important center of trade and commerce during the Middle Ages. The city played a significant role in the development of Russia, particularly in the fields of literature, art, and architecture.

ARCHITECTURE AND LANDMARKS

The city is home to many beautiful churches, monasteries, and other architectural marvels. The most famous landmark in Yaroslavl is the Spassky Monastery, which is a UNESCO World Heritage site. This beautiful complex, built in the 16th century, includes a stunning cathedral, bell tower, and other historic buildings.

Another noteworthy attraction is the Church of Elijah the Prophet, which is a beautiful example of Russian Baroque architecture. The church is famous for its stunning frescoes and iconography, which are considered to be among the best in Russia.

CULTURE AND ENTERTAINMENT

Yaroslavl is known for its rich cultural heritage, and there are many museums and galleries in the city that showcase its history and art. The Yaroslavl Art Museum, for example, houses an impressive collection of Russian art from the 18th to the 20th century.

In addition to its cultural offerings, Yaroslavl also offers many opportunities for outdoor recreation. The city is surrounded by beautiful forests and parks, and the Volga River provides plenty of opportunities for boating, fishing, and other water-based activities.

CONCLUSION

In conclusion, Yaroslavl city is a destination that offers a wealth of history, culture, and natural beauty. It is a perfect place to explore for those who want to experience a more authentic and less touristy side of Russia. With its stunning architecture, rich cultural heritage, and opportunities for outdoor recreation, Yaroslavl is a city that is not to be missed.

HRADEC KRALOVE, CZECH REPUBLIC

Located in the northeast of the Czech Republic, Hradec Kralove City is a historic town that offers a unique blend of modern and traditional elements. From its stunning architecture to its vibrant cultural scene, there is no shortage of things to see and do in this charming city.

GETTING TO HRADEC KRALOVE CITY

If you're coming from Prague, you can take a direct train to Hradec Kralove City that runs several times a day. Alternatively, you can also reach the city by bus, which offers a cheaper option but may take longer.

HISTORICAL LANDMARKS

Hradec Kralove City boasts a rich history, evident in its numerous historical landmarks. The most notable of these is the Cathedral of the Holy Spirit, which dates back to the 14th century and features stunning Gothic architecture. Another must-see attraction is the White Tower, a medieval fortification that offers breathtaking views of the city from its observation deck.

CULTURAL SCENE

Aside from its historical landmarks, Hradec Kralove City is also known for its vibrant cultural scene. The city hosts several festivals and events throughout the year, including the Summer of Culture festival, which features a variety of music and theater performances. Additionally, the city is home to several museums and art galleries, showcasing the works of local and international artists.

LOCAL CUISINE

No visit to Hradec Kralove City is complete without trying out the local cuisine. The city's traditional dishes include smažený sýr, which is deep-fried cheese, and knedlíky, a type of dumpling that is often served with meat and gravy. For dessert, try the trdelník, a sweet pastry that is rolled around a stick and roasted over an open flame.

PARKS AND GARDENS

If you're looking to unwind and escape the hustle and bustle of the city, head to one of Hradec Kralove's many parks and gardens. The largest of these is the East Bohemian Museum Garden, which features a beautiful rose garden and a small lake. Other notable parks include the Velké náměstí Park and the Šimkovy Sady Park.

FINAL THOUGHTS

Hradec Kralove City is a hidden gem in the Czech Republic, offering a unique blend of history, culture, and natural beauty. Whether you're interested in exploring the city's historical landmarks, indulging in local cuisine, or simply relaxing in one of its many parks, there is something for everyone in this charming city.

FARO, PORTUGAL

Faro is a charming coastal city located in the southernmost region of Portugal, known for its stunning beaches, historic landmarks, and vibrant culture. The city is an excellent destination for those looking to immerse themselves in the local culture and explore the rich history and traditions of this beautiful region.

HISTORICAL LANDMARKS

One of the main attractions of Faro is its rich history, which can be seen in the city's many historic landmarks. Visitors can explore the ancient Roman walls that once protected the city, or visit the stunning Cathedral of Faro, which dates back to the 13th century. Other notable landmarks include the Nossa Senhora da Assuncao Convent, the Municipal Museum of Faro, and the Arco da Vila, a beautiful triumphal arch that serves as the entrance to the historic center.

BEACHES

Faro is also famous for its stunning beaches, which are among the best in the country. The Praia de Faro is the most popular beach in the city, with its golden sands and crystal-clear waters. Visitors can also explore the quieter and more secluded Ilha Deserta, which is only accessible by boat and is perfect for those looking for a more secluded and tranquil beach experience.

LOCAL CULTURE

Faro is a vibrant city with a rich culture and traditions. Visitors can immerse themselves in the local culture by visiting the many traditional markets, where they can sample delicious local foods and wines. The city also hosts many cultural events throughout the year, including music festivals, art exhibitions, and traditional fairs.

NATURAL BEAUTY

In addition to its historical landmarks and beautiful beaches, Faro is also home to stunning natural beauty. Visitors can explore the Ria Formosa Natural Park, a protected wetland area that is home to a diverse range of wildlife, including flamingos and dolphins. The park also features many hiking and cycling trails, making it an excellent destination for outdoor enthusiasts.

CONCLUSION

Faro is a unique and beautiful city that offers something for everyone, from its rich history and stunning beaches to its vibrant culture and natural beauty. Whether you're looking for a relaxing beach vacation or an immersive cultural experience, Faro is a destination that should not be missed.

NORWICH, ENGLAND

Norwich is a beautiful city located in the East of England, known for its medieval architecture, cultural events, and rich history. Despite being often overshadowed by bigger cities like London or Edinburgh, Norwich is a hidden gem that offers visitors a unique and authentic English experience.

GETTING TO NORWICH

Norwich is well-connected by train and bus, making it easily accessible from other parts of the UK. The city also has its own airport, with flights to and from several European destinations.

EXPLORING THE CITY

Norwich's city center is compact and easily walkable, with many of its main attractions located within a short distance of each other. Visitors can start by exploring the city's medieval heritage by visiting Norwich Castle, which houses a museum with exhibits on the city's history, art, and culture. Another must-see attraction is Norwich Cathedral, an impressive building with a rich history that dates back to the 11th century.

For those interested in shopping and dining, Norwich has plenty of options, including independent shops, markets, and restaurants. The city also has a vibrant nightlife scene, with many pubs, bars, and clubs that cater to all tastes.

CULTURAL EVENTS

Norwich is known for its cultural events, including the Norfolk and Norwich Festival, a 17-day celebration of arts and culture that takes place every May. The city also hosts the Norwich Fringe Festival, a grassroots festival that showcases local talent in theater, music, and comedy.

OUTDOOR ACTIVITIES

Norwich has plenty of outdoor activities for those who enjoy nature and the great outdoors. The city is surrounded by beautiful countryside, including the Norfolk Broads, a network of rivers and lakes that is popular for boating and fishing. Visitors can also explore the Norfolk Coast Area of Outstanding Natural Beauty, which offers stunning views and plenty of opportunities for hiking, cycling, and birdwatching.

CONCLUSION

Norwich is a hidden gem that offers visitors a unique and authentic English experience. With its medieval architecture, cultural events, and outdoor activities, the city has something to offer everyone. Whether you're interested in history, art, or nature, Norwich is definitely worth a visit.

OHRID, NORTH MACEDONIA

Ohrid is a small city situated in the southwestern part of North Macedonia. It is a place that is not very well-known to the world, but it is a true gem of the Balkans. With its stunning natural beauty, rich history, and unique culture, Ohrid has everything that a traveler could want.

THE HISTORY OF OHRID

Ohrid has a long and fascinating history that dates back to the ancient times. It was founded by the Illyrian tribe of Enkeleida, and later it became an important center of the Macedonian Empire. During the Roman Empire, Ohrid was an important military and trading center.

In the Middle Ages, Ohrid became a center of Orthodox Christianity and an important cultural and artistic center. Many churches and monasteries were built during this period, and some of them still exist today. In the 10th century, the famous Ohrid Literary School was founded, which played an important role in the development of Slavic literature and culture.

NATURAL BEAUTY

Ohrid is situated on the shore of Lake Ohrid, which is one of the oldest and deepest lakes in Europe. The lake is crystal clear and has a unique ecosystem with many endemic species of plants and animals. The surrounding mountains and forests provide a stunning backdrop to the lake, making it a perfect place for hiking and outdoor activities.

Ohrid also has many beautiful beaches, where visitors can enjoy swimming and sunbathing. The most famous beach is the Gradiste Beach, which is located near the center of the city.

CULTURE AND TRADITIONS

Ohrid has a unique culture and traditions that are deeply rooted in its history and geography. The city has a diverse population, with Macedonians, Albanians, and other ethnic groups living together in harmony.

One of the most important cultural events in Ohrid is the Ohrid Summer Festival, which takes place every summer. The festival features a variety of music, theater, and dance performances, as well as exhibitions and workshops.

Another important tradition in Ohrid is the Ohrid pearl. The Ohrid pearl is a type of jewelry that is made from the scales of the Ohrid trout, which is found only in Lake

Ohrid. The Ohrid pearl is a symbol of the city and a unique souvenir for visitors.

CONCLUSION

Ohrid is a hidden gem in the Balkans that is waiting to be discovered. With its stunning natural beauty, rich history, and unique culture, Ohrid is a perfect destination for travelers who want to experience something new and different. Whether you are interested in history, nature, or culture, Ohrid has something for everyone.

WUPPERTAL, GERMANY

Are you looking for a unique and charming destination in Germany that is off the beaten track? Look no further than Wuppertal city, a hidden gem nestled in the Bergisches Land region. This picturesque city is known for its world-renowned suspension monorail, rich industrial history, and stunning natural scenery. Let's explore why Wuppertal should be on your travel itinerary.

GETTING THERE

Located in the North Rhine-Westphalia region, Wuppertal is easily accessible by train from major cities like Düsseldorf and Cologne. Alternatively, you can fly into Düsseldorf International Airport and take a short train ride to Wuppertal.

THE SUSPENSION MONORAIL

One of the main attractions of Wuppertal is the Suspension Monorail, or Schwebebahn, which runs through the city center. This unique mode of transportation has been in operation since 1901 and is a symbol of the city. Take a ride on the monorail and enjoy panoramic views of the city while passing over the Wupper River.

INDUSTRIAL HERITAGE

Wuppertal has a rich industrial history, and you can explore this heritage at the Wuppertal Industrial Museum. Housed in a former factory building, the museum showcases the city's industrial past with exhibits on textiles, toolmaking, and printing.

NATURE AND PARKS

Despite its urban location, Wuppertal is also known for its stunning natural scenery. Take a stroll through the Botanischer Garten Wuppertal, a botanical garden with over 4,000 plant species, or visit the Wuppertaler Schwebebahn Kaiserwagen, a cable car that takes you through the scenic Wupper Valley.

CULTURAL HIGHLIGHTS

Wuppertal also boasts a thriving arts and culture scene, with several theaters and museums. The Von der Heydt Museum is home to an impressive collection of art from the 19th and 20th centuries, while the Wuppertal Opera hosts world-class performances.

CONCLUSION

Wuppertal city may not be on everyone's radar, but it is certainly worth a visit for those seeking a unique and charming destination in Germany. From the world-famous Suspension Monorail to the city's rich industrial heritage and stunning natural scenery, there is something for everyone in Wuppertal. So pack your bags and get ready to explore this hidden gem!

RUSE, BULGARIA

Bulgaria is a country that is not yet well-known among travelers, but its cities are filled with hidden gems waiting to be discovered. One such city is Ruse, located on the northern bank of the Danube River. Ruse is often referred to as Bulgaria's "Little Vienna" because of its elegant architecture and rich cultural history.

THE ARCHITECTURE

Ruse is home to some of the most beautiful architecture in Bulgaria. The city's most famous landmark is the Ruse Opera House, which was built in 1898 and is considered to be one of the most beautiful buildings in the country. Other notable buildings include the Regional Museum of History, which houses artifacts from the Thracian and

Roman periods, and the House of Kaliopa, a stunning mansion that now serves as a museum.

CULTURAL SCENE

Ruse is also home to a vibrant cultural scene. The city has a number of theaters, including the Ivan Vazov National Theater and the Youth Theater. Ruse is also known for its music scene, with a number of local bands and performers playing in bars and clubs throughout the city.

NATURAL BEAUTY

Ruse is surrounded by beautiful countryside, and there are plenty of opportunities to explore the great outdoors. The city is located on the Danube River, and there are plenty of opportunities to take a boat tour or go fishing. The Rusenski Lom Nature Park is also nearby, offering hiking trails and stunning views of the local landscape.

GETTING AROUND

Ruse is a small city, and it's easy to get around on foot. There are also buses and taxis available for those who prefer not to walk.

FINAL THOUGHTS

If you're looking for a hidden gem in Bulgaria, Ruse is definitely worth a visit. With its stunning architecture, vibrant cultural scene, and beautiful natural surroundings, there's something for everyone in this charming city.

ZADAR, CROATIA

Zadar is a charming coastal city located on the Dalmatian coast of Croatia, known for its rich history, stunning natural beauty, and vibrant cultural scene. This hidden gem is often overlooked by tourists, but those who venture to Zadar will be rewarded with a truly unforgettable experience. In this article, we will explore some of the best things to do and see in Zadar, Croatia.

HISTORICAL SITES

Zadar has a rich history, and there are many historical sites to explore in the city. One of the most iconic landmarks is the Church of St. Donatus, a magnificent 9th-century church that is considered one of the finest examples of Byzantine architecture in the world. The Roman Forum is another must-visit site, which dates back to the 1st century BC and is one of the largest and best-preserved forums in Croatia.

NATURAL BEAUTY

Zadar is home to some of the most stunning natural landscapes in Croatia, such as the Paklenica National Park, which is located just 45 minutes from the city. This park is a paradise for nature lovers, with stunning mountain scenery, hiking trails, and crystal-clear rivers. For those who love the sea, the nearby Kornati Islands are a must-visit destination, with over 140 uninhabited islands and islets that are perfect for swimming, snorkeling, and sunbathing.

FOOD AND DRINK

Croatian cuisine is a delicious blend of Mediterranean and Central European influences, and Zadar is no exception. Visitors can enjoy traditional Croatian dishes such as fresh seafood, grilled meats, and hearty stews at local restaurants, paired with a glass of local wine or beer. The city is also famous for its Maraschino liqueur, a sweet cherry liqueur that has been produced in Zadar for over 200 years.

CULTURAL EVENTS

Zadar has a vibrant cultural scene, with numerous festivals and events throughout the year. One of the most popular is the Zadar Summer Festival, which takes place from June to September and features a wide range of music, theater, and dance performances. The city is also home to several museums and galleries, including the Museum of Ancient Glass, which houses an impressive collection of Roman glassware.

CONCLUSION

Zadar is a truly unique and unforgettable destination that offers something for everyone, whether you are interested in history, nature, food, or culture. With its stunning natural beauty, rich history, and vibrant cultural scene, Zadar is a hidden gem that should not be missed. So why not pack your bags and start planning your trip to this wonderful city today?

HUESCA, SPAIN

Located in the heart of the Aragon region of northern Spain, Huesca is a city with a rich history, cultural heritage, and beautiful landscapes. Known for its medieval architecture, stunning churches, and picturesque streets, Huesca is a must-visit destination for those who want to experience the beauty of Spain beyond its popular cities.

GETTING TO HUESCA

Huesca is easily accessible by car, bus, or train. The nearest airport is in Zaragoza, which is about an hour and a half away by car. The city is also well-connected to other major cities in Spain by train and bus.

DISCOVERING THE HISTORY

Huesca is steeped in history, dating back to the Roman era. The city has a number of ancient landmarks that are worth exploring, including the Cathedral of Saint Mary, the Castle of Montearagón, and the Romanesque Church of San Pedro el Viejo. Visitors can also stroll through the city's narrow streets and admire the medieval architecture that still stands today.

IMMERSING IN THE CULTURE

Apart from its historical significance, Huesca is also known for its rich culture. The city hosts a number of cultural events throughout the year, including the International Film Festival of Huesca, the San Lorenzo Festival, and the Carnival of Huesca. Visitors can also enjoy traditional Spanish cuisine and sample local wines at the city's many restaurants and bars.

EXPLORING THE OUTDOORS

Huesca is surrounded by breathtaking landscapes that are perfect for outdoor activities. The Pyrenees Mountains, which are just a short drive away, offer hiking, skiing, and mountaineering opportunities. The nearby Mallos de Riglos rock formations are also popular among rock climbers.

CONCLUSION

With its rich history, vibrant culture, and stunning landscapes, Huesca is a hidden gem in northern Spain that is waiting to be discovered. Whether you're a history buff, a foodie, or an outdoor enthusiast, Huesca has something for everyone. So, the next time you're planning a trip to Spain, make sure to include Huesca on your itinerary.

FRIBOURG, SWITZERLAND

If you're looking for an off-the-beaten-path destination in Europe, look no further than Fribourg, Switzerland. Tucked away in the country's picturesque countryside, Fribourg is a charming city with a rich history, stunning architecture, and a vibrant cultural scene.

HISTORY AND ARCHITECTURE

Fribourg dates back to the Middle Ages, and its Old Town is a testament to its rich history. The city's medieval architecture is well-preserved, and wandering the narrow streets and alleys is like stepping back in time. Highlights include the Gothic-style St. Nicholas Cathedral and the 15th-century Town Hall, which features an ornate façade with colorful murals.

CULTURE AND FESTIVALS

Fribourg is a university town, and the student population adds to the city's lively atmosphere. The city is also home to several museums, including the Art and History Museum, which features works from the Middle Ages to the present day. Fribourg is known for its festivals, including the Fribourg International Film Festival, the St. Nicholas

Fair, and the Folkloric Parade, which takes place every 10 years.

FOOD AND DRINK

Switzerland is known for its cheese, and Fribourg is no exception. The city is home to the famous Gruyère cheese, which is made from milk produced in the surrounding mountains. Visitors can sample the cheese at the local dairy, as well as in restaurants throughout the city. Fribourg is also known for its chocolate, and visitors can indulge in Swiss chocolate at local chocolatiers.

OUTDOOR ACTIVITIES

Fribourg is located in the Swiss countryside, and there are plenty of outdoor activities to enjoy. Hiking is a popular pastime, and the nearby Swiss Alps offer breathtaking views. The city is also situated on the Sarine River, and visitors can enjoy a scenic boat ride or try their hand at fishing.

CONCLUSION

Fribourg is a hidden gem in the heart of Europe, offering visitors a glimpse into Swiss history and culture. With its medieval architecture, vibrant cultural scene, and stunning countryside, Fribourg is the perfect destination for travelers looking for something off the beaten path.

DURHAM, ENGLAND

Durham is a city steeped in history, culture, and stunning architecture. Nestled in the northeast of England, Durham is a city that is often overlooked by tourists but has plenty to offer for those looking for a unique travel experience.

HISTORY AND ARCHITECTURE

One of the most impressive landmarks in Durham is the Durham Cathedral, a UNESCO World Heritage site that dates back to the 11th century. The cathedral's breathtaking Gothic architecture is a sight to behold, and visitors can also explore the adjacent Durham Castle, which has served as a Norman fortress and a residential palace for the bishops of Durham.

CULTURE AND ARTS

Durham is a city that celebrates its heritage through various cultural events and festivals. The Durham Book Festival, which takes place in October, attracts writers and book lovers from around the world. The Durham International Brass Festival, which happens every two years in July, showcases brass bands from around the globe. The city also has several art galleries and theaters that offer a diverse range of cultural events throughout the year.

NATURE AND OUTDOOR ACTIVITIES

Nature lovers will be pleased to know that Durham is surrounded by stunning countryside and nature reserves. The Durham Heritage Coast is a scenic stretch of coastline that offers breathtaking views of the North Sea. Visitors can also explore the Durham Dales, a picturesque area of rolling hills, valleys, and rivers that is popular with hikers and cyclists.

FOOD AND DRINK

Durham is home to several award-winning restaurants and pubs that serve up delicious local cuisine. The city has a thriving food and drink scene, and visitors can sample local delicacies such as Durham lamb, Stottie cakes, and Durham gin.

CONCLUSION

Durham is a city that has something for everyone. Whether you're interested in history, culture, nature, or food, Durham has plenty to offer. With its stunning architecture, cultural events, and beautiful countryside, Durham is a must-visit destination for anyone traveling to the northeast of England.

RENNES, FRANCE

Rennes is the capital of Brittany, a region located in the northwest of France. It is a vibrant city that boasts a rich cultural heritage and a lively student scene. Whether you are a history buff, a foodie, or a party animal, Rennes has something for everyone. In this travel guide, we will take you on a journey to explore the charming city of Rennes.

HISTORIC OLD TOWN

The historic old town of Rennes is a must-visit for any traveler. The city's rich history is evident in the medieval architecture of the buildings, narrow streets, and charming squares. The Place des Lices is a bustling market square where you can sample local delicacies, such as crepes and galettes. The Rue du Chapitre is another highlight of the old town, lined with half-timbered houses that date back to the 15th century.

REMARKABLE MUSEUMS

Rennes is home to some of France's most remarkable museums. The Musée des Beaux-Arts is a must-visit for art lovers, with its impressive collection of works from the 14th century to the present day. The Musée de Bretagne is another gem, where you can learn about the history and culture of Brittany. The Ecomusée du Pays de Rennes is an open-air museum that showcases the region's rural heritage and traditional crafts.

LOCAL CUISINE

Brittany is renowned for its gastronomy, and Rennes is no exception. The city is home to numerous restaurants and cafes that offer a variety of traditional dishes, such as the famous galettes and crepes. La Saint-Georges is a popular spot for crepes, while Le Bistrot de la Cité is known for its modern take on Breton cuisine. Don't forget to try the local cider and beer, which are brewed using traditional methods.

VIBRANT NIGHTLIFE

Rennes has a vibrant nightlife, thanks to its large student population. The Rue de la Soif is a street lined with bars and clubs that come alive at night. La Suite is a popular nightclub that attracts a young and lively crowd. Le Chantier is a quirky bar that serves craft beer and hosts live music events. Whether you prefer a laid-back evening or a wild night out, Rennes has something to offer.

CONCLUSION

Rennes is a charming city that offers a unique blend of history, culture, cuisine, and nightlife. Whether you are visiting for a day or a week, you are sure to be enchanted by its beauty and vibrancy. So why not plan your next trip to Rennes and discover this hidden gem for yourself?

OSTRAVA, CZECH REPUBLIC

Ostrava is a city located in the northeastern part of the Czech Republic, known for its rich industrial history, cultural diversity, and unique attractions. Despite being one of the lesser-known cities in Europe, Ostrava has a lot to offer for travelers looking to explore something off the beaten path.

GETTING TO OSTRAVA

The best way to get to Ostrava is by flying into the Leoš Janáček Ostrava Airport, which serves several international destinations. Alternatively, you can also arrive by train from major cities such as Prague and Vienna.

INDUSTRIAL HERITAGE

One of the most prominent features of Ostrava is its industrial heritage. In the past, the city was a hub for mining and steel production, and remnants of this industrial past can still be seen today. Visitors can take a tour of the city's industrial landmarks, such as the Dolni Vitkovice complex, which is now a cultural center and museum.

CULTURAL DIVERSITY

Ostrava is also known for its cultural diversity, with a large population of Polish and Roma communities living alongside Czechs. This diversity is reflected in the city's food, music, and art scenes, making it a fascinating destination for cultural immersion. Visitors can explore the Silesian Ostrava Castle, which houses the Moravian-Silesian Museum and showcases the history of the region.

NATURAL BEAUTY

Despite its industrial past, Ostrava also boasts natural beauty. The city is surrounded by forests and green spaces, making it a perfect destination for nature lovers. The Ostravice River offers opportunities for water sports and fishing, and the nearby Beskydy Mountains provide breathtaking views and hiking trails.

CONCLUSION

In conclusion, Ostrava may not be the first city that comes to mind when planning a trip to Europe, but it is certainly worth a visit. With its unique blend of industrial heritage, cultural diversity, and natural beauty, Ostrava is a hidden gem waiting to be discovered.

SOPRON, HUNGARY

Sopron, a charming city located in western Hungary, is often overlooked by travelers in favor of Budapest or Vienna. However, this hidden gem offers a unique and authentic experience for those who take the time to visit.

LOCATION AND HISTORY

Sopron is situated in close proximity to the Austrian border, making it a perfect stop for those traveling between Vienna and Budapest. The city has a rich history, with evidence of human settlement dating back to the Roman Empire. Over the centuries, Sopron has been occupied by various powers, including the Ottoman Empire and the Habsburgs, before eventually becoming part of Hungary.

THINGS TO DO

Despite its relatively small size, Sopron has plenty to offer visitors. The city's old town is filled with historic buildings, such as the Firewatch Tower and the Gothic-style St. Michael's Church. Walking around the cobblestone streets and admiring the architecture is a delightful experience in itself.

Sopron is also home to several museums, including the Fabricius House, which showcases the city's rich history, and the Pharmacy Museum, which gives insight into the evolution of medicine over the centuries.

For nature lovers, the Lővérek forest offers hiking trails and stunning views of the surrounding countryside. And of course, no visit to Sopron is complete without trying some of the local wines, which are produced in the nearby vineyards.

FOOD AND DRINK

Hungarian cuisine is known for its hearty and flavorful dishes, and Sopron is no exception. The city is home to several traditional Hungarian restaurants, where you can try dishes such as goulash, paprikash, and chimney cake. And with the city's proximity to Austria, you'll also find plenty of Austrian-style cafes and pastries.

As for drinks, Sopron is famous for its wine, particularly the local Kékfrankos variety. Wine tastings are available at several wineries in the area, and you can also sample local wines at many of the restaurants and cafes in the city.

CONCLUSION

If you're looking for a unique and authentic travel experience in Hungary, Sopron is definitely worth a visit. With its rich history, charming old town, and delicious food and wine, this hidden gem is sure to delight any traveler.

NIZHNY NOVGOROD, RUSSIA

If you're planning a trip to Russia, you may have already heard of Moscow and St. Petersburg, but there's another city you don't want to miss: Nizhny Novgorod. Located about 250 miles east of Moscow, this city has a rich history, stunning architecture, and plenty of things to do.

HISTORY

Nizhny Novgorod was founded in the 13th century and was an important trade center for centuries. In the 19th century, it became a major industrial city and was a hub for the Soviet Union's military and aerospace industries during the Cold War.

ARCHITECTURE

One of the highlights of Nizhny Novgorod is its architecture. The city has numerous historical buildings, including the Nizhny Novgorod Kremlin, a fortress that dates back to the 16th century. The Kremlin's walls and towers offer spectacular views of the city.

Another must-see attraction is the Chkalov Staircase, a staircase that connects the upper and lower parts of the city. It has 560 steps and was named after Valery Chkalov, a famous Soviet aviator.

THINGS TO DO

Nizhny Novgorod has plenty of activities for tourists. If you're interested in history, you can visit the Nizhny Novgorod State Historical and Architectural Museum Reserve, which has exhibits on the city's history and culture.

If you prefer outdoor activities, there are several parks and nature reserves in the area, including the Nizhny

Novgorod National Park, where you can go hiking, camping, and fishing.

The city also has a vibrant nightlife, with many bars, clubs, and restaurants to choose from.

CONCLUSION

Nizhny Novgorod may not be as well-known as some of Russia's other cities, but it's definitely worth a visit. With its rich history, stunning architecture, and plenty of things to do, it's a hidden gem that should be on every traveler's itinerary.

COMO, ITALY

If you're planning a trip to Northern Italy, be sure to add Como to your list of must-visit destinations. Nestled on the shores of Lake Como, this picturesque city boasts stunning scenery, fascinating history, and a vibrant culture. Here's what you need to know to make the most of your visit.

GETTING TO COMO

Como is located in the Lombardy region of Northern Italy, just 45 minutes north of Milan. The city is easily accessible by train or car, and there are several airports nearby, including Milan's Malpensa Airport.

EXPLORING THE CITY

Como's historic center is a charming maze of cobblestone streets, medieval buildings, and quaint shops and cafes. You'll want to spend plenty of time exploring the city's many landmarks, including the magnificent Como Cathedral, the 14th-century Broletto Palace, and the imposing Porta Torre gateway.

LAKE COMO

Of course, no visit to Como would be complete without a trip to the lake itself. Take a stroll along the promenade, rent a boat, or hop on a ferry to explore the surrounding towns and villages. You'll be treated to breathtaking views of the Alps and the crystal-clear waters of the lake.

FOOD AND WINE

Italy is known for its delicious food and wine, and Como is no exception. Sample local specialties like risotto with perch, missoltini (dried and salted shad fish), and panettone, a sweet bread traditionally eaten during the holidays. Wash it all down with a glass of locally-produced wine, such as the fruity and refreshing Valcalepio Bianco.

SHOPPING

Como is famous for its silk production, and the city is home to several shops and factories where you can purchase high-quality silk products. Whether you're in the market for a scarf, tie, or even a full outfit, you're sure to find something to suit your taste.

CONCLUSION

From its stunning natural scenery to its rich history and culture, Como has something for everyone. Whether you're looking to relax by the lake, indulge in delicious food and wine, or immerse yourself in the city's vibrant atmosphere, you won't be disappointed by this charming Northern Italian gem.

BANSKO, BULGARIA

Bansko is a charming town situated in the southwestern part of Bulgaria, nestled in the foothills of the Pirin Mountains. This picturesque city attracts visitors from all over the world, who come to explore its rich history, stunning natural beauty, and exciting outdoor activities.

HISTORY AND CULTURE

Bansko has a fascinating history, dating back to the Roman Empire. The city has been a center of commerce and culture for centuries, and its charming old town is filled with historic buildings, cobblestone streets, and traditional Bulgarian architecture. Visitors can explore the historic churches and museums, such as the Holy Trinity Church, the Bansko Museum, and the Nikola Vaptsarov

Museum, which showcase the city's rich cultural heritage.

NATURAL BEAUTY AND OUTDOOR ACTIVITIES

Bansko is also renowned for its natural beauty, which offers a range of outdoor activities for visitors to enjoy. The Pirin Mountains are a UNESCO World Heritage site, known for their rugged peaks, deep gorges, and crystal-clear lakes. Visitors can go hiking, skiing, and snowboarding in the winter months, or take a leisurely stroll through the mountains in the summer. Bansko is also home to a range of hot springs and spa resorts, where visitors can relax and rejuvenate after a day of adventure.

FOOD AND DRINK

Bansko is a food lover's paradise, with a range of traditional Bulgarian cuisine on offer. Visitors can sample local specialties such as kavarma, a hearty meat stew, and banitsa, a savory pastry filled with cheese and spinach. The city is also home to a range of bars and restaurants, offering local wines, beers, and spirits.

ACCOMMODATION

Bansko offers a range of accommodation options, from budget-friendly hostels to luxury hotels and resorts. Visitors can choose to stay in the heart of the old town, with its traditional Bulgarian architecture and charming streets, or in the modern ski resorts on the outskirts of the city.

CONCLUSION

Bansko is a must-visit destination for anyone looking to explore Bulgaria's natural beauty and rich cultural heritage. With its historic old town, stunning mountain scenery, and exciting outdoor activities, Bansko has something to offer every traveler. Whether you're looking for adventure, relaxation, or a bit of both, Bansko is the perfect place to experience the best of Bulgaria.

KAVALA, GREECE

Nestled on the northeastern coast of Greece, Kavala city is a hidden gem for travelers looking to experience the rich history and natural beauty of the region. From its ancient ruins and picturesque waterfront to its vibrant cultural scene and bustling markets, there is something for everyone in this charming city.

THE CITY'S HISTORY

With a history dating back to the 7th century BC, Kavala city has a wealth of historical sites for visitors to explore. One of the most popular attractions is the ancient Roman aqueduct, which still stands today as a testament to the city's engineering prowess. The nearby archaeological museum showcases artifacts from the city's various eras, including ancient Greek and Roman artifacts, Byzantine icons, and Ottoman-era relics.

NATURAL WONDERS

In addition to its rich history, Kavala city is also known for its stunning natural beauty. Visitors can take a scenic drive up to the Panagia peninsula, where they can enjoy panoramic views of the Aegean Sea and the surrounding mountains. The city is also home to several beaches, including Batis Beach and Tosca Beach, which are perfect for swimming, sunbathing, and water sports.

CULTURAL EXPERIENCES

Kavala city is known for its vibrant cultural scene, with numerous events and festivals throughout the year. The most famous of these is the Kavala Carnival, which takes place in February and attracts thousands of visitors from around the world. The city also has a thriving music scene, with live performances by local and international artists at venues such as the Municipal Music Hall and the Kavala International Music Festival.

SHOPPING AND DINING

For those looking to indulge in some retail therapy, Kavala city has a variety of shops and markets selling everything from handmade souvenirs to fresh produce. The city's most famous market, the Imaret Market, is a must-visit for foodies, offering a wide variety of local delicacies such as fresh seafood, olives, and traditional sweets.

FINAL THOUGHTS

Whether you're interested in history, natural beauty, or cultural experiences, Kavala city has something for everyone. With its friendly locals, delicious cuisine, and stunning surroundings, this hidden gem is well worth a visit on your next trip to Greece.

AARHUS, DENMARK

Aarhus is a vibrant city in Denmark, known for its rich history, culture, and stunning architecture. This coastal city offers something for everyone, whether you're interested in art, history, or nature. Here's a guide to help you plan your trip to Aarhus and make the most of your time in this beautiful city.

GETTING TO AARHUS

Aarhus is easily accessible by plane, train, or car. The city has its own airport, Aarhus Airport, which has daily flights to and from various European cities. The train station is located in the city center and offers regular connections to Copenhagen, Aalborg, and other major cities in Denmark. If you prefer to drive, Aarhus is well connected to the rest of Denmark via highways and roads.

EXPLORING THE CITY

Aarhus is a compact city, so it's easy to explore on foot or by bike. The city center is home to many of Aarhus' top attractions, including the Old Town, the ARoS Aarhus Art Museum, and the Aarhus Cathedral. Take a stroll through the charming Latin Quarter, where you'll find colorful houses, quaint cafes, and artisan shops.

For a taste of Denmark's rich history, head to the Moesgaard Museum, where you can explore the country's Viking past and learn about its early inhabitants. The Aarhus Botanical Gardens and the Marselisborg Forests are perfect for nature lovers and offer beautiful green spaces for walking and picnicking.

LOCAL CULTURE

Aarhus is a city that celebrates art and culture. The ARoS Aarhus Art Museum is a must-visit attraction, housing a collection of contemporary and modern art. For live performances, head to the Musikhuset Aarhus, where you can catch concerts, theater shows, and dance performances.

If you're visiting in the summer, be sure to check out the Aarhus Festival, a week-long celebration of art, music, and culture. The festival features street performers, live music, and art installations throughout the city.

LOCAL CUISINE

No trip to Aarhus is complete without sampling some of the city's delicious local cuisine. From fresh seafood to traditional Danish dishes, there's something for everyone. Head to the Aarhus Street Food Market, where you can sample a variety of local and international dishes.

For a more upscale dining experience, book a table at one of the city's Michelin-starred restaurants, such as Frederikshøj or Substans. And if you're a beer lover, be sure to visit some of Aarhus' microbreweries, such as Mikkeller Aarhus or Aarhus Bryghus.

FINAL THOUGHTS

Aarhus is a city that truly has it all - from history and culture to nature and cuisine. Whether you're a first-time visitor or a seasoned traveler, there's always something new to discover in this charming Danish city. So pack your bags, book your tickets, and get ready for an unforgettable trip to Aarhus.

PECS, HUNGARY

When it comes to exploring the best of Hungary, Budapest is often the top destination that comes to mind. However, those who venture beyond the country's capital will discover a hidden gem in the southwestern region of Hungary - Pecs City. This charming city offers a unique blend of history, culture, and natural beauty that's worth exploring.

HISTORY AND CULTURE

Pecs City is a city steeped in history and culture that dates back to the Roman Empire. The city's historic center is a UNESCO World Heritage Site that features stunning examples of Roman, Turkish, and Baroque architecture. Visitors can explore the iconic Mosque Church of Pasha Qasim, the beautiful Zsolnay Cultural Quarter, and the historic Vasarely Museum.

NATURAL BEAUTY

Beyond its rich history and culture, Pecs City is surrounded by beautiful natural landscapes that are perfect for outdoor enthusiasts. The city is home to the Mecsek Hills, a range of low mountains that offer breathtaking views of the surrounding countryside. Visitors can also explore the beautiful Danube-Drava National Park, which is home to a diverse range of flora and fauna.

CULINARY DELIGHTS

Hungarian cuisine is known for its hearty, flavorful dishes that are made with locally sourced ingredients. Pecs City is no exception, offering a wide range of traditional Hungarian dishes that are sure to delight foodies. Visitors can try local specialties like goulash soup, stuffed cabbage rolls, and chimney cake at one of the many cozy restaurants in the city.

FESTIVALS AND EVENTS

Pecs City is known for its lively festivals and events that take place throughout the year. One of the most popular events is the Pécs Spring Festival, which features a diverse range of music, dance, and theater performances. Visitors can also attend the Zsolnay Light Festival, which showcases stunning light installations and 3D projections throughout the city.

GETTING TO PECS

Pecs is easily accessible by train or bus from Budapest, and the journey takes approximately 2.5 to 3 hours. The city also has an airport with flights to several European destinations.

CONCLUSION

Pecs City may not be as well-known as Budapest, but it offers a unique and unforgettable travel experience that's well worth exploring. Whether you're interested in history and culture, natural beauty, culinary delights, or lively festivals and events, Pecs City has something for everyone. So, pack your bags and start planning your trip to this hidden gem in Hungary today!

COSENZA, ITALY

Nestled in the Calabrian region of Southern Italy, Cosenza is a hidden gem waiting to be discovered by travelers. This vibrant city boasts a rich history, stunning architecture, and delicious cuisine, making it an ideal destination for those looking to experience authentic Italian culture.

HISTORY AND CULTURE

Cosenza has a rich history that dates back to ancient times. The city was founded by the ancient Greeks and later became an important center of learning during the Roman Empire. Today, visitors can explore the city's many historical sites, including the ancient Roman bridge, the Norman Castle, and the Cathedral of Cosenza.

The city also has a thriving cultural scene, with numerous museums, theaters, and art galleries showcasing the works of local artists. Visitors can also enjoy traditional Calabrian music and dance performances, which are held throughout the year.

ARCHITECTURE

Cosenza's architecture is a mix of ancient and modern styles, creating a unique blend of old-world charm and contemporary design. The historic center of the city is home to many beautiful buildings, including the Palazzo Arnone, the Church of San Francesco di Paola, and the Church of San Domenico.

FOOD AND DRINK

Cosenza is known for its delicious cuisine, which is influenced by the region's agricultural heritage and proximity to the sea. Visitors can sample traditional dishes like 'nduja, a spicy sausage made with pork, and cipolla rossa di Tropea, a sweet red onion grown in the region. Local wines, such as Cirò and Greco di Bianco, are also a must-try.

CONCLUSION

Cosenza is a wonderful destination for travelers looking to explore the rich history and culture of Southern Italy. With its beautiful architecture, delicious cuisine, and lively cultural scene, there is something for everyone in this hidden gem of a city. So why not plan a trip to Cosenza today and experience the best that Southern Italy has to offer?

LUGANO, SWITZERLAND

Lugano is a beautiful city located in the southern part of Switzerland, known for its breathtaking views of the Alps, scenic lakeside promenades, and vibrant cultural scene. This picturesque city is the perfect destination for travelers who want to experience the best of Switzerland.

LOCATION AND GETTING THERE

Lugano is situated in the Italian-speaking canton of Ticino in southern Switzerland. It is easily accessible by train or car from major Swiss cities like Zurich, Geneva, and Bern. The city also has its own airport, Lugano Airport, which offers direct flights to several European cities.

SIGHTS AND ACTIVITIES

Lugano offers plenty of activities and sights for travelers to explore. The city has a rich cultural heritage and is home to many museums, art galleries, and historic landmarks. The city's historic center is particularly charming, with narrow streets and colorful buildings that give it a distinctly Italian feel.

For nature lovers, Lugano offers numerous opportunities to enjoy the outdoors. The city is surrounded by mountains and is located on the shore of Lake Lugano, providing plenty of opportunities for hiking, biking, and water sports. The Parco Civico, a large public park, is also a great place to relax and enjoy the views.

FOOD AND DRINK

Swiss cuisine is renowned for its delicious cheese, chocolate, and wine, and Lugano is no exception. The city has a vibrant food scene, with plenty of restaurants and cafes serving traditional Swiss dishes as well as international cuisine. Visitors should try the local specialties like risotto, polenta, and the famous Ticino Merlot wine.

ACCOMMODATIONS

Lugano has a range of accommodations to suit all budgets and preferences. Visitors can choose from luxury hotels, boutique hotels, and budget-friendly hostels. Some of the best hotels in the city offer stunning views of Lake Lugano and the surrounding mountains.

CONCLUSION

Lugano is a hidden gem in Switzerland that should not be missed. With its stunning natural beauty, rich cultural heritage, and delicious food and drink, it is the perfect destination for travelers who want to experience the best of Switzerland. Whether you're looking to explore the city's history and culture, enjoy the great outdoors, or simply relax and take in the views, Lugano has something for everyone.

ESKILSTUNA, SWEDEN

Eskilstuna is a quaint and charming city located in the heart of Sweden. Known for its rich history, natural beauty, and modern amenities, it is a perfect destination for travelers looking for a unique experience.

THE HISTORY OF ESKILSTUNA

Eskilstuna has a long and fascinating history that dates back to the Viking era. The city was founded in the 10th century and was once an important trading hub. Over the years, it has evolved into a center for innovation and industry, with a strong focus on sustainability.

SIGHTS AND SOUNDS

There is no shortage of things to see and do in Eskilstuna. Visitors can explore the city's rich cultural heritage by visiting its many museums and historical sites, including the Rademachersmedjorna museum and the Munktellmuseet. The city is also home to several beautiful parks and nature reserves, such as the Hjälmare kanal and the Vilsta nature reserve, where visitors can enjoy hiking, biking, and other outdoor activities.

LOCAL CUISINE

Eskilstuna is known for its diverse and flavorful cuisine, with a range of restaurants and cafes that offer traditional Swedish dishes as well as international cuisine.

Some of the most popular local dishes include meatballs, gravlax, and lingonberry jam. For those with a sweet tooth, the city is home to several bakeries and pastry shops that offer delicious pastries and desserts.

SHOPPING AND ENTERTAINMENT

Eskilstuna offers a range of shopping and entertainment options for visitors. The city has several modern shopping centers, including the Tuna Park and the Eskilstuna City shopping center, where visitors can find a range of international and local brands. There are also several cinemas, theaters, and music venues that offer a range of entertainment options.

CONCLUSION

Overall, Eskilstuna is a beautiful and charming city that offers a unique travel experience. With its rich history, natural beauty, and modern amenities, it is a perfect destination for travelers who want to explore the best of Sweden. Whether you're interested in culture, nature, or cuisine, Eskilstuna has something to offer for everyone.

SKOPJE, NORTH MACEDONIA

Skopje is the capital and largest city of North Macedonia, located in the heart of the Balkans. Although it is not as popular as some of its neighboring cities like Athens or Istanbul, Skopje has a rich history and a vibrant cultural scene that make it a must-visit destination for any traveler.

HISTORY AND CULTURE

Skopje has a long and complex history that dates back to ancient times. The city was a part of the Roman Empire, the Byzantine Empire, the Ottoman Empire, and the Kingdom of Yugoslavia, which has left a diverse mix of architectural styles and cultural influences throughout the city.

One of the most iconic landmarks of Skopje is the Stone Bridge, a historic Ottoman-era bridge that spans the Vardar River and connects the old town with the new town. Other must-see attractions include the Kale Fortress, the Old Bazaar, and the Skopje City Museum, which showcases the city's rich history and cultural heritage.

FOOD AND NIGHTLIFE

Skopje is known for its delicious cuisine, which features a blend of Balkan, Mediterranean, and Middle Eastern flavors. Some of the most popular dishes include grilled meats, stuffed peppers, and burek, a savory pastry filled with cheese, meat, or vegetables.

When it comes to nightlife, Skopje has a vibrant and lively scene with numerous bars, clubs, and cafes. The Old Bazaar is a popular spot for enjoying a drink and socializing with locals, while the city center is home to several trendy clubs that stay open late into the night.

OUTDOOR ACTIVITIES

Skopje is also a great destination for outdoor enthusiasts, with several parks and natural areas located within the city and surrounding region. The Matka Canyon is a popular spot for hiking and kayaking, while the Mount Vodno offers stunning views of the city and is accessible via a cable car.

CONCLUSION

Skopje is a hidden gem in the Balkans, offering a unique blend of history, culture, and outdoor activities. Whether you're interested in exploring the city's rich heritage or enjoying its vibrant nightlife, Skopje has something for everyone. So why not add this charming city to your travel itinerary and discover all that it has to offer?

PORTO SANTO, PORTUGAL

Porto Santo City is a beautiful destination located on the island of Porto Santo in Madeira, Portugal. The city is known for its stunning natural beauty, charming ambiance, and serene beaches. In this article, we will take a closer look at what makes Porto Santo City an ideal location for travelers looking for a relaxing getaway.

GETTING TO THE CITY

The island of Porto Santo is located about 43 kilometers northeast of the island of Madeira, and the only way to get to Porto Santo City is by ferry or by small plane from Funchal, the capital of Madeira. The journey by ferry takes about 2.5 hours, while the flight from Funchal takes only about 15 minutes.

DISCOVERING THE CITY

Once you arrive in Porto Santo City, you will immediately notice the serene and laid-back atmosphere that characterizes the island. The city is home to several historic sites, including the Christopher Columbus Museum, which tells the story of Columbus's connection to the island.

One of the city's main attractions is its stunning golden sandy beaches. The beaches in Porto Santo City are some of the most beautiful in Portugal, with crystal clear waters and breathtaking scenery. The most famous beach in the city is the Porto Santo Beach, which stretches for nine kilometers along the island's southern coast.

EXPLORING THE ISLAND

Porto Santo City is an excellent starting point for exploring the rest of the island. One of the most popular activities is hiking the island's scenic trails, which offer stunning views of the island's natural beauty. You can also explore the island's flora and fauna by visiting the Porto Santo Nature Reserve.

Another must-visit attraction is Pico do Facho, the island's highest peak. From the summit, visitors can enjoy panoramic views of the entire island and the surrounding ocean. Additionally, there are several charming villages scattered throughout the island that are worth visiting, including Vila Baleira, Camacha, and Fonte da Areia.

CONCLUSION

In conclusion, Porto Santo City is a hidden gem that offers travelers a peaceful and relaxing vacation in a stunning natural setting. Whether you're interested in history, nature, or simply lounging on the beach, Porto Santo City has something to offer everyone. So, pack your bags, book your tickets, and get ready to experience the beauty of Porto Santo City.

ST. GALLEN, SWITZERLAND

Nestled in the northeastern region of Switzerland lies the charming city of St. Gallen. With a rich history dating back to the 7th century, St. Gallen is known for its impressive baroque architecture, world-class museums, and breathtaking scenery. Whether you're a history buff, an art enthusiast, or simply looking for a peaceful escape, St. Gallen has something to offer everyone.

GETTING THERE AND AROUND

St. Gallen is easily accessible by train or car. The nearest airport is Zurich International Airport, which is just over an hour away by train. Once you arrive in St. Gallen, the city's efficient public transportation system makes it easy to get around. Buses and trams run regularly throughout the city, and taxis are also readily available.

RICH HISTORY

St. Gallen's history is closely tied to its famous monastery, which dates back to the 8th century. The St. Gallen Abbey Library, which houses over 170,000 rare books and manuscripts, is a must-visit for history buffs. The Abbey Library is also home to one of the world's oldest surviving globes, dating back to 1507. Other notable historical sites include the St. Gallen Cathedral, a stunning example of baroque architecture, and the Abbey of St. Gall, a UNESCO World Heritage site.

ART SCENE

St. Gallen is also home to a thriving art scene. The Kunstmuseum St. Gallen, located in a beautiful 19th-century villa, features an impressive collection of modern and contemporary art. The Museum im Lagerhaus, housed in a former brewery, showcases works by local artists. For a unique cultural experience, be sure to visit the Textile Museum, which explores the history of textile production in St. Gallen.

NATURAL BEAUTY

St. Gallen's stunning natural scenery is not to be missed. The city is surrounded by rolling hills, verdant forests, and pristine lakes. For a breathtaking view of the city and the surrounding landscape, hike up to the Drei Weieren, a trio of lakes nestled in the hills above St. Gallen. The Wildpark Peter & Paul, a wildlife park located just outside the city, is a great place to spot native animals such as deer, ibex, and wolves.

CONCLUSION

In conclusion, St. Gallen is a hidden gem that offers something for every type of traveler. With its rich history, vibrant art scene, and stunning natural beauty, St. Gallen is a destination that should not be missed. Whether you're visiting for a day or a week, St. Gallen is sure to leave a lasting impression.

ÅLESUND, NORWAY

Nestled on the west coast of Norway, Ålesund is a picturesque city known for its Art Nouveau architecture, rich history, and stunning natural surroundings. With its charming atmosphere and unique character, Ålesund is a must-visit destination for anyone looking to experience the best of Norway.

HISTORY AND CULTURE

Founded in 1848, Ålesund is a relatively young city, but it has a rich and fascinating history. In 1904, a devastating fire destroyed most of the city, but it was quickly rebuilt in the Art Nouveau style that has come to define its character. Today, visitors can explore the city's many Art Nouveau buildings, as well as its museums and galleries that showcase its cultural heritage.

NATURAL BEAUTY

Ålesund is situated on the coast of Norway, surrounded by mountains and fjords that offer breathtaking views and opportunities for outdoor adventures. Visitors can take a hike up the Aksla viewpoint for panoramic views of the city and the surrounding landscape, or take a boat tour to explore the nearby fjords.

ACTIVITIES AND ATTRACTIONS

In addition to its stunning natural surroundings and rich cultural heritage, Ålesund offers a variety of activities and attractions for visitors of all ages. The city is home to several parks, gardens, and beaches that are perfect for relaxing and enjoying the scenery. Visitors can also explore the city's many shops, restaurants, and cafes, which offer a range of local and international cuisine and souvenirs.

CONCLUSION

If you're planning a trip to Norway, be sure to include Ålesund on your itinerary. With its unique combination of history, culture, and natural beauty, this coastal gem is sure to leave a lasting impression on you.

MODENA, ITALY

Modena is a charming city located in the Emilia-Romagna region of Northern Italy. While often overshadowed by its more famous neighbors such as Bologna and Florence, Modena has plenty to offer travelers looking for an authentic Italian experience. Here are some of the highlights of this hidden gem.

FOOD AND DRINK

Emilia-Romagna is known as the culinary capital of Italy, and Modena is no exception. The city is famous for its balsamic vinegar, Parmigiano-Reggiano cheese, and Lambrusco wine. Make sure to visit the Mercato Albinelli, the city's largest indoor market, to sample local delicacies and pick up some ingredients for a picnic in one of Modena's many parks.

ARCHITECTURE AND HISTORY

Modena is steeped in history, and its architecture reflects the city's rich past. The Romanesque Modena Cathedral is a must-see, with its intricate carvings and soaring bell tower. Another must-visit is the Ducal Palace, a former residence of the Este family that now houses the Military Academy of Modena. The Palace's Baroque façade and elegant interior are sure to impress.

CULTURE AND ART

Modena has a vibrant cultural scene, with a variety of museums and galleries to explore. The Galleria Estense houses an impressive collection of Renaissance and Baroque art, while the Museum of Enzo Ferrari celebrates the life and work of the famous Italian automobile designer. The Teatro Comunale is also worth a visit, with its opulent interior and world-class performances.

CONCLUSION

Modena may not be as well-known as some of its neighbors, but it is a city that rewards the intrepid traveler. With its delicious food and drink, fascinating history and architecture, and thriving cultural scene, Modena is a hidden gem waiting to be discovered.

SOCHI, RUSSIA

Located on the coast of the Black Sea in southwestern Russia, Sochi is a popular tourist destination that boasts stunning natural landscapes, vibrant nightlife, and a rich cultural heritage. Here's everything you need to know before you set off on your Sochi adventure.

GETTING THERE

Sochi is easily accessible by air, with the Sochi International Airport serving several international and domestic airlines. Alternatively, you can take a train or bus from Moscow, St. Petersburg, or other major cities in Russia.

WHERE TO STAY

Sochi offers a wide range of accommodation options to suit all budgets, from luxury resorts and hotels to hostels and budget guesthouses. For a more authentic experience, consider staying in one of the many traditional Russian dachas, which are small cottages or country houses.

THINGS TO DO

Sochi has plenty of activities to keep visitors entertained. One of the city's most popular attractions is the Sochi National Park, which features stunning waterfalls, hiking trails, and scenic overlooks. If you're looking for something more adventurous, try skiing or snowboarding at Krasnaya Polyana, one of the country's top ski resorts.

For those interested in history and culture, Sochi is home to several museums, including the Stalin Museum and the Art Museum of Sochi. The city also hosts several festivals throughout the year, such as the Sochi Jazz Festival and the Kinotavr Film Festival.

NIGHTLIFE AND ENTERTAINMENT

Sochi has a lively nightlife scene with numerous bars, clubs, and restaurants. The city is also home to several casinos, including the Sochi Casino and Resort, which offers a range of table games and slot machines.

FOOD AND DRINK

Sochi is known for its delicious cuisine, which features fresh seafood, locally grown produce, and traditional Russian dishes. Some of the city's must-try dishes include khachapuri, a savory cheese-filled pastry, and borscht, a hearty beet soup. The region is also home to several wineries and breweries, producing some of Russia's finest wines and beers.

FINAL THOUGHTS

Sochi is a city with something for everyone, whether you're looking for outdoor adventure, cultural experiences, or just a relaxing beach vacation. With its stunning natural beauty, rich history, and vibrant nightlife, Sochi is a destination that should be on every traveler's bucket list.

MONSCHAU, GERMANY

Monschau city is a picturesque town located in the western part of Germany, near the Belgian border. The town is known for its well-preserved half-timbered houses, narrow streets, and beautiful natural surroundings. Monschau is a popular tourist destination, offering visitors an opportunity to experience the charm of a medieval town while enjoying modern amenities.

GETTING THERE

Monschau is easily accessible by car, train, and bus. The closest airports are in Cologne and Dusseldorf, both of which are less than two hours away by car. If you're traveling by train, the nearest station is in Aachen, which is about 30 minutes away. Once you arrive in Monschau, you can explore the town on foot or by bike.

THINGS TO DO

Monschau offers a variety of activities for visitors of all ages. You can start by exploring the old town, which is filled with half-timbered houses, quaint cafes, and charming shops. The town is also home to several museums, including the Monschau Castle Museum and the Red House Museum, which offer insights into the town's history and culture.

If you're looking for outdoor activities, Monschau has plenty to offer. The town is situated in the Eifel National

Park, which is home to hiking and biking trails, as well as stunning natural scenery. You can also go canoeing or kayaking on the Rur River, which runs through the town.

WHERE TO STAY

Monschau offers a variety of accommodations, from cozy guesthouses to luxurious hotels. If you want to stay in the heart of the old town, there are several charming guesthouses and bed and breakfasts to choose from. If you prefer more modern amenities, there are also several hotels and resorts outside of the town center.

FOOD AND DRINK

Monschau is known for its local cuisine, which includes hearty soups, stews, and sausages. The town is also home to several breweries and distilleries, where you can sample local beers and spirits. There are several restaurants and cafes throughout the town, offering a variety of international and regional cuisine.

CONCLUSION

Monschau is a charming town that offers visitors a glimpse into Germany's rich history and culture. Whether you're interested in exploring the old town, hiking in the national park, or sampling local cuisine, Monschau has something for everyone. So if you're planning a trip to Germany, be sure to put Monschau on your list of must-visit destinations.

LA ROCHELLE, FRANCE

La Rochelle is a picturesque port city located on the west coast of France, in the region of Nouvelle-Aquitaine. With its stunning architecture, rich history, and beautiful beaches, La Rochelle is a popular destination for travelers from all around the world. In this article, we will explore some of the top attractions and things to do in La Rochelle, to help you plan your next vacation.

HISTORY AND CULTURE

La Rochelle has a rich history that dates back to the 10th century. The city was an important hub for trade and commerce during the Middle Ages, and it played a significant role in the Protestant Reformation in the 16th century. The city's rich history is reflected in its many historic landmarks and museums, including the Old Port, the Saint-Nicolas Tower, and the Natural History Museum.

ATTRACTIONS

One of the top attractions in La Rochelle is the Old Port, which is a bustling hub of activity with its many cafes, restaurants, and shops. The port is also home to several historic landmarks, including the three towers of La Rochelle: the Saint-Nicolas Tower, the Tour de la Chaîne, and the Tour de la Lanterne.

Another must-see attraction in La Rochelle is the Aquarium, which is one of the largest aquariums in Europe. The aquarium is home to over 12,000 marine animals and offers visitors a unique opportunity to explore the fascinating world of marine life.

BEACHES

La Rochelle is also home to several beautiful beaches, including Plage des Minimes, which is the largest beach in the city. The beach is popular with tourists and locals alike, and it offers a range of activities, including swimming, sunbathing, and water sports.

FOOD AND DRINK

La Rochelle is famous for its delicious seafood, which can be found in many of the city's restaurants and cafes. Some of the most popular dishes include moules-frites (mussels with fries), oysters, and seafood platters. The city is also known for its wine, particularly the white wines of the nearby Île de Ré.

CONCLUSION

La Rochelle is a charming city with something to offer every traveler. Whether you're interested in history and culture, beaches, or food and drink, this city has it all. So why not plan your next vacation in La Rochelle and discover the beauty and charm of this stunning seaside city?

TRENTO, ITALY

If you are looking for an off-the-beaten-path destination in Northern Italy, Trento is the perfect choice. This small city, located in the Trentino-Alto Adige region, has a rich history, stunning architecture, and a vibrant cultural scene. Here are some reasons why Trento should be on your travel itinerary.

HISTORY

Trento has a long and fascinating history, dating back to the Roman Empire. The city was an important center of trade and commerce in the Middle Ages, and it played a crucial role in the Council of Trent, which reformed the Catholic Church in the 16th century. You can explore Trento's history by visiting its museums, such as the Tridentine Museum of Natural Sciences, the Museum of Modern and Contemporary Art, and the Museum of Trento.

ARCHITECTURE

Trento's architecture is a beautiful blend of medieval and Renaissance styles. The city's most iconic building is the Buonconsiglio Castle, which was built in the 13th century and served as the residence of the prince-bishops of Trento. Other notable landmarks include the Trento Cathedral, the Church of Santa Maria Maggiore, and the Palazzo Pretorio.

CULTURAL SCENE

Trento has a lively cultural scene, with numerous festivals and events throughout the year. One of the highlights is the Trento Film Festival, which showcases the best documentaries and films about mountains, adventure, and exploration. The city also hosts the International Festival of Economics, which brings together leading economists, policymakers, and business leaders from around the world to discuss pressing global issues.

CUISINE

Trento is located in the heart of the Italian Alps, and its cuisine reflects the region's mountainous landscape. The city is known for its hearty dishes, such as canederli (dumplings made with bread, cheese, and bacon), polenta (a type of cornmeal porridge), and strudel (a pastry filled with apples or other fruits). Trento is also home to some excellent wineries, producing world-class wines such as Trentodoc (a sparkling wine made with Chardonnay and Pinot Noir grapes).

CONCLUSION

Trento may not be as well-known as other Italian cities, but it has plenty to offer for travelers who are looking for a unique and authentic experience. With its rich history, stunning architecture, lively cultural scene, and delicious cuisine, Trento is a hidden gem waiting to be discovered.

KLAIPEDA, LITHUANIA

If you're looking for a unique and culturally rich travel destination, consider Klaipeda, Lithuania. Located on the Baltic Sea, this historic city has something for everyone.

HISTORY AND ARCHITECTURE

Klaipeda is one of the oldest cities in Lithuania, with a history dating back to the 7th century. The city has been influenced by many different cultures over the years, including German, Swedish, and Russian, resulting in a diverse blend of architecture and cultural influences.

The city's Old Town is a must-visit for architecture lovers, with its cobbled streets and historic buildings, including the 18th-century Simon Dach House, and the neo-Gothic-style Klaipeda Clock and Watch Museum. The city also boasts a number of impressive churches, including the St. John the Baptist Church, which dates back to the 17th century.

CULTURE AND ENTERTAINMENT

Klaipeda is known for its vibrant arts and culture scene. The city is home to numerous museums and galleries, including the Klaipeda Picture Gallery and the Lithuanian Sea Museum. The city also hosts a number of annual festivals and events, such as the Klaipeda Castle Jazz Festival and the Sea Festival, which celebrates the city's maritime heritage.

FOOD AND DRINK

Lithuanian cuisine is hearty and flavorful, with dishes like cepelinai (potato dumplings stuffed with meat or cheese) and kugelis (a potato pudding) being must-tries. Klaipeda has a range of restaurants and cafes serving traditional Lithuanian cuisine, as well as international fare.

NATURE AND ADVENTURE

Klaipeda is surrounded by natural beauty, from the Curonian Spit National Park to the Nemunas Delta Regional Park. Visitors can explore the area by hiking, cycling, or taking a boat tour. The city is also home to the Dolphinarium, where visitors can watch dolphins perform and learn about marine conservation.

CONCLUSION

Klaipeda is a fascinating travel destination, with a rich history, vibrant culture, delicious food, and stunning natural surroundings. Whether you're interested in history, art, or outdoor adventure, this Lithuanian city has something to offer.

BYDGOSZCZ, POLAND

Located in the heart of Northern Poland, Bydgoszcz is a vibrant and charming city that offers a unique blend of modernity and history. The city is known for its picturesque Old Town, diverse cultural offerings, and lush green spaces. Whether you're a history buff, an art enthusiast, or just looking for a fun weekend getaway, Bydgoszcz has something for everyone.

HISTORY AND CULTURE

Bydgoszcz is steeped in history and culture, with a rich past that dates back to the 10th century. The city was once an important trade and commerce center, and its architecture reflects its diverse influences over the centuries. The Old Town is a must-see destination, with its colorful buildings, cobbled streets, and charming cafes. The city also boasts several museums and galleries that showcase the city's history and cultural heritage, including the Leon Wyczolkowski Regional Museum, which houses a collection of Polish art and artifacts.

OUTDOOR ACTIVITIES

If you're looking for outdoor activities, Bydgoszcz has plenty to offer. The city is situated on the banks of the Brda River, which offers opportunities for kayaking and canoeing. The nearby forests and parks are also great for hiking and cycling. Bydgoszcz is also home to several parks and gardens, including the Mill Island Park, which is a popular spot for picnics and outdoor concerts.

FOOD AND DRINK

Polish cuisine is hearty and flavorful, and Bydgoszcz is no exception. The city is home to several restaurants and cafes that serve traditional Polish dishes, as well as international cuisine. Pierogi, a type of Polish dumpling, is a must-try dish, and Bydgoszcz has several restaurants that specialize in this delicious treat. The city is also known for its craft beer scene, with several breweries and beer gardens that offer a wide variety of locally brewed beers.

GETTING THERE

Bydgoszcz is easily accessible by air, rail, or road. The city has its own airport, which offers flights to several European destinations. Bydgoszcz is also well connected by rail, with regular trains to Warsaw, Gdansk, and other cities. If you're driving, the city is located on the A1 highway, which connects it to the rest of Poland.

CONCLUSION

Bydgoszcz may not be as well-known as some of Poland's other cities, but it's a hidden gem that's well worth a visit. Whether you're interested in history, culture, or outdoor activities, Bydgoszcz has something for everyone. So why not plan a trip and discover this charming city for yourself?

ALGHERO, ITALY

Alghero is a charming coastal town located on the northwest coast of the island of Sardinia, Italy. Known for its picturesque medieval old town, stunning beaches, and vibrant culture, Alghero has become a popular destination for travelers seeking a taste of authentic Italian charm. Here is a closer look at what makes Alghero a must-see destination.

HISTORY AND CULTURE

Alghero's history dates back to the prehistoric Nuragic civilization, and the town has been influenced by various cultures over the centuries, including the Romans, Byzantines, and Catalans. The town's Catalan heritage is particularly evident in its architecture and language, as well as in its cuisine, which features fresh seafood and traditional Catalan dishes.

OLD TOWN

The heart of Alghero is its stunning medieval old town, which is surrounded by ancient walls and towers. Visitors can wander through narrow cobblestone streets lined with colorful buildings, browse boutique shops selling local handicrafts and souvenirs, and stop for a drink or a meal at one of the many cafes and restaurants.

BEACHES

Alghero is also known for its beautiful beaches, which offer crystal-clear waters and pristine white sand. Some of the most popular beaches include Maria Pia, Le Bombarde, and Lazzaretto, which are all easily accessible from the town center.

ACTIVITIES AND EVENTS

There is always something happening in Alghero, with a variety of events and festivals taking place throughout the year. In particular, the town is known for its vibrant nightlife, with plenty of bars and clubs to keep visitors entertained well into the night. Other popular activities include hiking in the nearby countryside, exploring the nearby Neptune's Grotto, and taking a boat tour along the coast.

CONCLUSION

With its rich history, charming old town, stunning beaches, and vibrant culture, Alghero is a destination that has something to offer for everyone. Whether you're interested in history and culture, outdoor activities, or simply relaxing on the beach, Alghero is a destination that should not be missed.

TALLINN, ESTONIA

Tallinn is the capital of Estonia, a small country situated in Northern Europe. It is a charming city that boasts a rich history, stunning architecture, and a vibrant cultural scene. Tallinn's unique mix of old-world charm and modern amenities makes it a popular destination for tourists from around the world. In this article, we'll take a closer look at what makes Tallinn a must-visit destination.

EXPLORING THE OLD TOWN

Tallinn's Old Town is a UNESCO World Heritage site and is known for its picturesque cobblestone streets, medieval buildings, and historic landmarks. You can spend hours wandering through the winding alleyways, admiring the well-preserved Gothic and Baroque architecture. Be sure to visit the iconic Tallinn Town Hall, which dates back to the 14th century and is one of the oldest town halls in Europe.

CULINARY DELIGHTS

Tallinn is home to some of the best restaurants in Estonia, offering a range of cuisines from traditional Estonian dishes to international fare. The city is particularly famous for its seafood, with restaurants like the F-Hoone and the Seafood Bar offering some of the freshest catches of the day.

NIGHTLIFE

Tallinn has a vibrant nightlife scene with something to suit every taste. From cozy pubs to trendy nightclubs, the city offers a wide range of entertainment options. The city's Old Town is particularly popular for its nightlife, with many bars and pubs lining the streets.

ART AND CULTURE

Tallinn is a hub for art and culture, with numerous galleries, museums, and theaters throughout the city. The Kumu Art Museum is a must-visit for art enthusiasts, showcasing both contemporary and traditional Estonian art. The Estonian National Opera and Ballet Theater is another popular attraction, hosting world-class performances throughout the year.

NATURAL BEAUTY

Tallinn is surrounded by stunning natural scenery, with many parks, forests, and beaches within easy reach of the city. The Kadriorg Park is a popular destination, with its beautiful gardens, lakes, and palaces. The nearby Pirita Beach is also a great spot to relax and soak up the sun during the summer months.

FINAL THOUGHTS

Tallinn is a city that truly has something for everyone. From its historic Old Town to its vibrant nightlife, cultural attractions, and natural beauty, there's no shortage of things to see and do in this charming city. Whether you're a history buff, foodie, art lover, or nature enthusiast, Tallinn is a destination that should definitely be on your travel bucket list.

TRABZON, TURKEY

Trabzon is a beautiful city located on the eastern coast of the Black Sea in Turkey. The city has a rich history and culture, with beautiful natural scenery and plenty of historical sites to explore. In this article, we will take a closer look at what makes Trabzon such a special destination for travelers.

HISTORY AND CULTURE

Trabzon has a long and fascinating history, dating back to ancient times. It was an important trading center during the Byzantine Empire and played a significant role in the silk trade between China and Europe. The city has also been ruled by various empires and civilizations, including the Greeks, Romans, and Ottomans.

As a result of this rich history, Trabzon has a unique culture and architecture that reflects its diverse influences. Visitors can explore beautiful historical sites such as the Hagia Sophia Museum, the Trabzon Castle, and the Ataturk Mansion.

NATURAL BEAUTY

Trabzon is also known for its stunning natural scenery, including beautiful mountains, forests, and beaches. One of the most popular attractions is the Uzungol Lake, a serene lake surrounded by lush greenery and towering mountains. Visitors can take a hike around the lake or rent a boat for a relaxing ride.

Another must-see destination is the Sumela Monastery, located on a steep cliff in the Altindere National Park. The monastery dates back to the 4th century and is surrounded by breathtaking natural beauty.

LOCAL CUISINE

Trabzon is also famous for its delicious local cuisine, which features a variety of fresh seafood and traditional Turkish dishes. Visitors can try local specialties such as hamsi pilavı (anchovy pilaf), karalahana çorbası (kale soup), and kuymak (a type of cheesy polenta).

In addition to the food, Trabzon is also known for its tea culture. The city is surrounded by tea plantations, and visitors can enjoy a cup of traditional Turkish tea in one of the many tea gardens scattered throughout the city.

CONCLUSION

Trabzon is a destination that offers something for everyone, whether you are interested in history, nature, or food. With its unique culture and stunning scenery,

Trabzon is a jewel on Turkey's Black Sea coast that should not be missed.

SARANDA, ALBANIA

Saranda, a small coastal town located in southern Albania, is quickly gaining popularity as a must-visit destination for travelers seeking a combination of history, culture, and natural beauty. With its pristine beaches, crystal-clear waters, and lush greenery, Saranda offers visitors an unforgettable experience that combines both relaxation and adventure.

HISTORY AND CULTURE

Saranda has a rich history that dates back to ancient times. The city was once known as Onchesmos, and it was an important trading center in the ancient world. In the 5th century BC, it was conquered by the Greeks and later became part of the Roman Empire. Today, visitors can explore the ancient ruins of Butrint, a UNESCO World Heritage site located just a short distance from Saranda. Butrint contains the remains of a Greek acropolis, a Roman theater, and an early Christian basilica.

BEACHES AND NATURE

One of the main attractions of Saranda is its stunning beaches. The city is surrounded by clear blue waters, and there are plenty of beaches to choose from, including

Ksamil Beach, Mirror Beach, and Pasqyra Beach. Visitors can relax on the sandy beaches, swim in the crystal-clear waters, or enjoy water sports like snorkeling and kayaking.

Saranda is also known for its lush greenery and scenic views. Visitors can hike to Lekursi Castle, which offers breathtaking views of the city and the Ionian Sea. The Blue Eye, a natural spring located just outside of Saranda, is another popular attraction. The spring is named for its deep blue color, and visitors can swim in the cool, refreshing water.

FOOD AND DRINK

Saranda offers a variety of dining options, from traditional Albanian cuisine to international dishes. Seafood is a specialty in Saranda, and visitors can enjoy fresh catch from the local waters at one of the many seafood restaurants. Wine lovers will also appreciate the local wines, which are made from grapes grown in the nearby hills.

CONCLUSION

Saranda is a hidden gem in the Albanian Riviera, offering visitors a unique combination of history, culture, nature, and relaxation. With its stunning beaches, ancient ruins, and delicious cuisine, Saranda is quickly becoming a top destination for travelers seeking an authentic Balkan experience.

MAASTRICHT, NETHERLANDS

Nestled in the southernmost part of the Netherlands lies the city of Maastricht, known for its rich history, stunning architecture, and vibrant culture. This charming city is a perfect destination for those who want to immerse themselves in the Dutch way of life and explore the beauty of the Netherlands beyond Amsterdam.

A HISTORICAL OVERVIEW

Maastricht has a history that dates back to the Roman era, making it one of the oldest cities in the Netherlands. The city played a crucial role in European history, with the famous Treaty of Maastricht signed here in 1992, which led to the creation of the European Union. The city's strategic location on the banks of the Maas River made it an important center of trade and commerce throughout the centuries.

EXPLORING THE CITY

Maastricht is a city best explored on foot or by bike, with plenty of charming streets and picturesque squares to discover. The city is home to many historic landmarks, including the Basilica of Saint Servatius, which dates back to the 4th century. Another must-see attraction is the impressive fortress of St. Pieter, which was built in the 18th century to protect the city from invasion.

The city is also known for its excellent shopping, with a variety of high-end boutiques and unique local shops lining the streets. The bustling Markt square is a great place to start, with its lively market stalls selling everything from fresh produce to handmade crafts.

FOOD AND DRINK

No trip to Maastricht would be complete without indulging in the city's culinary delights. The local cuisine is heavily influenced by the neighboring countries of Belgium and Germany, with hearty stews, sausages, and Belgian waffles all popular dishes. For something sweet, try a slice of vlaai, a traditional Dutch fruit pie.

The city is also home to many excellent cafes and bars, with a lively nightlife scene that caters to all tastes. Whether you're in the mood for a cozy pub or a trendy cocktail bar, you'll find plenty of options to choose from.

FINAL THOUGHTS

Maastricht may not be as well-known as Amsterdam or Rotterdam, but it is a city that is definitely worth exploring. With its rich history, stunning architecture, and vibrant culture, it offers a unique and authentic Dutch experience that is sure to leave a lasting impression on any traveler. So, if you're looking for a new and exciting destination to add to your travel list, be sure to put Maastricht at the top.

MATERA, ITALY

If you're a traveler who is always on the lookout for unique and offbeat destinations, then Matera should be at the top of your list. Tucked away in the southern region of Italy, Matera is a charming and enchanting city that is steeped in history and culture. Here's everything you need to know about this hidden gem.

HISTORY AND CULTURE

Matera has a rich and fascinating history that spans over 30,000 years. The city is famous for its ancient cave dwellings, which are believed to be some of the oldest human settlements in Italy. These dwellings, known as Sassi, have been beautifully preserved and have been designated as a UNESCO World Heritage Site. In addition to the Sassi, Matera is also home to a number of stunning churches, museums, and palaces that showcase the city's rich cultural heritage.

EXPLORING THE CITY

The best way to explore Matera is on foot. The city's narrow alleyways and steep stairs make it a challenging but rewarding place to wander around. As you stroll through the streets, you'll come across a number of hidden gems, such as ancient churches, panoramic viewpoints, and local markets. Don't forget to sample the local cuisine while you're there, which includes delicious pasta dishes, fresh seafood, and flavorful wines.

ACCOMMODATION

If you're planning a trip to Matera, you'll find a range of accommodation options to suit all budgets. From luxurious hotels to charming bed and breakfasts, there's something for everyone. For a truly unique experience, consider staying in one of the Sassi cave dwellings that have been converted into stylish hotels and apartments.

WHEN TO GO

Matera can be visited year-round, but the best time to go is during the spring or fall when the weather is mild and the crowds are smaller. Summer can be hot and crowded, while winter can be chilly and rainy. If you're visiting in the summer, be sure to bring plenty of sunscreen and water.

FINAL THOUGHTS

Matera is a hidden gem that is waiting to be discovered. With its ancient history, charming streets, and delicious food, it's a destination that will leave a lasting impression on any traveler. So, what are you waiting for? Book your trip to Matera today and start exploring!

PLZEN, CZECH REPUBLIC

Plzen, located in the western region of the Czech Republic, is a historic city with a rich culture and fascinating architecture. Known as the birthplace of Pilsner beer, Plzen is also a UNESCO World Heritage Site and has numerous attractions to offer visitors.

GETTING TO PLZEN

Plzen is easily accessible by train or bus from Prague, the capital city of the Czech Republic. The journey takes approximately one hour by train and slightly longer by bus. Visitors can also fly into Prague's Vaclav Havel Airport and then take a bus or train to Plzen.

EXPLORING PLZEN

Plzen is a compact city that can easily be explored on foot. The city's historic center is home to stunning Gothic and Baroque architecture, including the Plzen Cathedral, which dates back to the 13th century. Visitors can also stroll through the colorful Renaissance-style houses in the city's square.

THE PILSNER URQUELL BREWERY

No visit to Plzen would be complete without a tour of the Pilsner Urquell Brewery. Founded in 1842, this brewery is the birthplace of Pilsner beer and offers visitors an opportunity to learn about the history and brewing process of this iconic beer. The tour includes a visit to the brewery's cellars, where visitors can taste unfiltered and unpasteurized Pilsner straight from the barrels.

THE GREAT SYNAGOGUE

Plzen is also home to the second-largest synagogue in Europe, the Great Synagogue. Built in the Moorish Revival style in 1893, the synagogue can accommodate up to 1,800 worshippers. The synagogue is open to visitors and offers an opportunity to learn about the Jewish history of Plzen.

THE BOHEMIAN FOREST

For visitors who enjoy the great outdoors, the Bohemian Forest is just a short drive from Plzen. This national park is home to diverse flora and fauna and offers a variety of hiking and cycling trails. Visitors can also enjoy fishing and kayaking in the park's lakes and rivers.

CONCLUSION

Plzen is a charming and historically rich city that offers something for everyone. Whether you're interested in beer, architecture, or outdoor adventures, Plzen is a must-visit destination in the Czech Republic.

BRIGHTON, ENGLAND

Brighton is a city located on the south coast of England. It is known for its vibrant and diverse culture, stunning beaches, and historic architecture. The city has something to offer for everyone, whether you are a history buff, a beach lover, or a foodie.

HISTORY AND CULTURE

Brighton has a rich history dating back to the 18th century when it was a popular seaside resort for the wealthy. The city was home to King George IV, who transformed the Royal Pavilion into a magnificent palace in the Indian style. Today, visitors can tour the palace and explore the rich history of the city at the Brighton Museum and Art Gallery.

Brighton is also a hub for contemporary arts, with numerous galleries and exhibitions showcasing the work of local and international artists. The city hosts the Brighton Fringe Festival, one of the largest fringe festivals in the world, featuring performances from over 5,000 artists across multiple venues.

BEACHES AND OUTDOOR ACTIVITIES

Brighton's beaches are some of the best in England, with a long promenade that stretches along the coast. Visitors can relax on the pebble beach, take a dip in the sea, or stroll along the pier. The pier has a range of attractions including an amusement park, arcades, and restaurants.

For those who love the outdoors, Brighton has plenty of options. The South Downs National Park is a short drive away, offering stunning hikes and cycling trails with panoramic views of the coast and countryside. Visitors can also take a boat tour to see the iconic chalk cliffs of Seven Sisters.

FOOD AND DRINK

Brighton is a food lover's paradise, with a diverse range of cuisine available. The city has a thriving food scene, with everything from street food to fine dining. The Brighton Food Festival takes place every year, featuring a range of food and drink stalls, cooking demonstrations, and tastings.

In addition to food, Brighton is also known for its vibrant nightlife. The city has a wide range of bars and clubs catering to all tastes, from indie music to electronic dance music.

CONCLUSION

Brighton is a vibrant and diverse city with a rich history, stunning beaches, and a thriving arts and culture scene. Whether you are a history buff, a beach lover, or a foodie, there is something for everyone in this charming city on the south coast of England.

SIGHISOARA, ROMANIA

Sighisoara is a medieval city located in the heart of Transylvania, Romania. This city is known for its well-preserved fortified walls, cobbled streets, and charming houses. It is one of the few inhabited medieval citadels in Europe and has been listed as a UNESCO World Heritage Site since 1999.

HISTORY OF SIGHISOARA

The city of Sighisoara was founded in the 12th century by German craftsmen and merchants known as the Saxons. The city grew to become an important center of commerce and culture in Transylvania. The old town of Sighisoara was built on a hilltop overlooking the Tarnava Mare River, providing strategic advantages in times of war.

THINGS TO SEE AND DO

Sighisoara has many sights and activities to offer. The Clock Tower Museum is a popular destination for tourists, as it provides a glimpse into the city's history and culture. Visitors can climb to the top of the tower to enjoy a panoramic view of the city.

Another must-see attraction is the Church on the Hill, which houses a collection of 16th-century frescoes and a crypt where notable figures from Sighisoara's past are buried.

Visitors can also take a stroll along the cobbled streets of the old town, which are lined with charming houses and restaurants serving traditional Romanian cuisine.

Sighisoara is also known for its annual medieval festival, which takes place in July and attracts thousands of visitors from around the world. The festival celebrates the city's medieval heritage with music, dance, and performances by actors dressed in medieval costumes.

GETTING TO SIGHISOARA

Sighisoara is easily accessible by train or car from major Romanian cities such as Bucharest, Cluj-Napoca, and Brasov. Visitors can also fly into the nearby airports in Targu-Mures or Sibiu and then take a bus or taxi to Sighisoara.

CONCLUSION

Sighisoara is a must-visit destination for anyone interested in history, culture, and medieval architecture. Its well-preserved citadel and charming old town offer visitors a glimpse into the past, while its vibrant cultural scene and lively festivals provide plenty of entertainment for modern-day travelers.

KOTOR, MONTENEGRO

Kotor City, located on the Adriatic coast in Montenegro, is a must-visit destination for anyone looking for a unique and picturesque travel experience. The city is known for its stunning natural beauty, rich history, and unique architecture. Here's why you should add Kotor City to your travel bucket list.

HISTORY

Kotor City has a long and fascinating history, dating back to the Roman era. Over the centuries, it has been ruled by various empires, including the Venetians, Austrians, and Ottomans. This has left a rich cultural and historical legacy, which is visible in the city's architecture, museums, and landmarks.

ARCHITECTURE

The city's architecture is a blend of different styles, including Gothic, Renaissance, and Baroque. The most famous landmark in Kotor City is the fortified Old Town, which was built by the Venetians in the 16th century. The Old Town is a UNESCO World Heritage Site and is famous for its narrow streets, squares, and stunning buildings.

NATURAL BEAUTY

Kotor City is nestled at the foot of a majestic mountain range and is surrounded by the stunning Bay of Kotor.

The bay is one of the most picturesque in the world, and it's easy to see why. The crystal-clear waters of the bay, combined with the lush greenery of the mountains, create a breathtaking vista that is truly unforgettable.

ACTIVITIES

There are plenty of activities to keep you busy in Kotor City. One of the most popular things to do is to take a walk along the city walls, which offer panoramic views of the city and the bay. You can also visit the various museums and art galleries in the city, which showcase the rich cultural heritage of the region. If you're feeling more adventurous, you can take a boat tour of the bay or go hiking in the mountains.

CONCLUSION

Kotor City is a beautiful and unique destination that should be on every traveler's bucket list. With its rich history, stunning architecture, and natural beauty, it offers something for everyone. Whether you're interested in history, culture, or outdoor activities, you're sure to find something to love in Kotor City.

AMIENS, FRANCE

If you're planning a trip to France and looking for a city that's not on the usual tourist trail, consider Amiens. Located in the northern region of Picardy, Amiens is a charming city that's rich in history, culture, and architecture.

GETTING TO AMIENS

The city is easily accessible by train from Paris, with a journey time of just over an hour. Alternatively, if you're driving, Amiens is conveniently located just off the A16 motorway.

EXPLORING AMIENS

One of the highlights of Amiens is its stunning Gothic cathedral. Built in the 13th century, the Notre-Dame d'Amiens is a UNESCO World Heritage Site and is one of the largest cathedrals in France. Its intricate facade and stunning stained-glass windows make it a must-see for any visitor to the city.

Another notable attraction in Amiens is the Hortillonnages, a series of gardens and canals located on the outskirts of the city. You can take a boat tour to explore the gardens and learn about their history and importance to the local community.

For art lovers, the Musée de Picardie is a must-visit. The museum houses an impressive collection of art and artifacts from the Picardy region, including works by famous artists such as Monet, Delacroix, and Corot.

FOOD AND DRINK

No trip to France would be complete without sampling some of the local cuisine, and Amiens has plenty to offer in this regard. One of the most famous local dishes is the macaron d'Amiens, a sweet almond-based pastry that's been made in the city for centuries.

For something more substantial, try the ficelle picarde, a savory crepe filled with ham, mushrooms, and cheese, or the flamiche aux poireaux, a leek and cheese tart that's a Picardy specialty.

CONCLUSION

Whether you're a history buff, an art lover, or just looking for a relaxing break away from the hustle and bustle of Paris, Amiens is definitely worth a visit. With its stunning cathedral, picturesque gardens, and delicious local cuisine, this hidden gem in northern France is sure to leave a lasting impression.

KURESSAARE, ESTONIA

Located on the stunning Saaremaa Island in Estonia, Kuressaare is a quaint city that offers visitors a perfect blend of historic charm and modern amenities. With its picturesque streets, ancient castle, and vibrant cultural scene, Kuressaare is a must-visit destination for anyone planning a trip to Estonia.

A HISTORIC AND CULTURAL HAVEN

Kuressaare is a city steeped in history and culture. One of the city's main attractions is its stunning castle, which dates back to the 14th century. The castle now houses a museum, where visitors can learn about the fascinating history of the island and the city.

The city is also home to a number of art galleries and museums, including the Saaremaa Museum and the Kuressaare Town Museum. These institutions offer visitors a glimpse into the island's rich cultural heritage and provide a deeper understanding of the city's past and present.

NATURAL BEAUTY

Kuressaare is situated on the southern coast of Saaremaa Island, and its location offers visitors an opportunity to explore the island's stunning natural beauty. The city is surrounded by pristine beaches, rugged coastline, and verdant forests, making it a paradise for nature lovers.

Visitors can take a leisurely stroll along the picturesque streets of the city, explore the beautiful parks and gardens, or head out into the countryside to enjoy hiking, biking, and bird-watching.

CULTURAL SCENE

Despite its small size, Kuressaare boasts a vibrant cultural scene. The city hosts a number of festivals and events throughout the year, including the Kuressaare Maritime Festival, the Saaremaa Opera Days, and the Kuressaare Chamber Music Days.

The city's many art galleries and theaters showcase the works of both local and international artists, and the city's restaurants and cafes offer a variety of cuisine options to suit any taste.

FINAL THOUGHTS

Kuressaare is a charming and historic city that offers visitors a perfect blend of culture, natural beauty, and modern amenities. Whether you're interested in exploring the city's rich history, enjoying the natural beauty of Saaremaa Island, or experiencing the vibrant cultural scene, Kuressaare has something for everyone.

RAVENNA, ITALY

Nestled in the Emilia-Romagna region of Italy, Ravenna is a city steeped in art, culture, and history. Known for its stunning Byzantine mosaics and UNESCO World Heritage Sites, Ravenna is a must-visit destination for anyone interested in architecture and art.

HISTORY AND CULTURE

Ravenna has a rich history that spans over 2,000 years. The city was once the capital of the Western Roman Empire and later served as the capital of the Byzantine Empire in Italy. As a result, the city is home to numerous architectural and artistic treasures, including eight UNESCO World Heritage Sites.

ARTISTIC TREASURES

One of the main attractions of Ravenna is its stunning Byzantine mosaics. These intricate works of art are made up of tiny pieces of colored glass and stone, arranged in intricate patterns and designs. Some of the most famous mosaics can be found in the Basilica di San Vitale, the Mausoleum of Galla Placidia, and the Baptistery of Neon.

Other notable artistic treasures in Ravenna include the Arian Baptistery, the Archiepiscopal Museum, and the National Museum of Ravenna. Visitors can spend hours admiring the beautiful works of art and learning about their historical and cultural significance.

PRACTICAL INFORMATION

Ravenna is easily accessible by train or car, and it is also served by an airport in nearby Bologna. The city is compact and walkable, making it easy to explore on foot. Visitors should plan to spend at least two or three days in Ravenna to fully appreciate all that it has to offer.

Accommodations in Ravenna range from budget-friendly hostels to luxury hotels, and there are also numerous restaurants and cafes serving traditional Italian cuisine. Visitors can also take advantage of Ravenna's proximity to other nearby cities, such as Bologna, Florence, and Venice, to plan a longer trip to Italy.

CONCLUSION

Ravenna is a true gem of Italy, offering visitors a unique blend of history, culture, and art. Whether you're an art enthusiast, history buff, or simply looking for a beautiful and relaxing place to visit, Ravenna is a must-see destination that will leave you in awe.

MONTPELLIER, FRANCE

Montpellier is a city located in the southern part of France, on the Mediterranean coast. It is the capital of the Hérault department and the seventh-largest city in the country. The city boasts a rich history, a diverse cultural scene, and a vibrant student population. In this article, we'll explore some of the highlights of Montpellier and why it's worth a visit.

HISTORY AND ARCHITECTURE

Montpellier has a long and fascinating history, dating back to the Middle Ages. The city was founded in the 10th century and grew rapidly during the 12th and 13th centuries, becoming an important center of trade and commerce. As a result, Montpellier has a rich architectural heritage, with numerous historic buildings and monuments to explore.

One of the city's most famous landmarks is the Place de la Comédie, a grand square in the heart of Montpellier. Here, you can find the Opéra Comédie, a beautiful 19th-century opera house, as well as numerous cafés and restaurants. Other notable buildings include the Saint-Pierre Cathedral, the Arc de Triomphe, and the Porte du Peyrou.

CULTURE AND ENTERTAINMENT

Montpellier is a vibrant and dynamic city, with a lively cultural scene that caters to a wide range of tastes. The city is home to numerous museums, galleries, and cultural institutions, including the Musée Fabre, which houses an impressive collection of European art from the 17th to the 20th centuries.

For music lovers, Montpellier offers a diverse range of concerts and performances, with venues such as the Zénith Sud and the Rockstore hosting major international acts. The city also hosts a number of festivals throughout the year, including the Festival de Radio France et Montpellier, which celebrates classical music, and the Montpellier Danse festival, which showcases contemporary dance.

FOOD AND DRINK

No trip to Montpellier would be complete without sampling the city's culinary delights. The local cuisine is characterized by its Mediterranean flavors, with an emphasis on fresh seafood, herbs, and spices. The city is home to numerous restaurants, cafés, and bars, serving everything from traditional French dishes to international cuisine.

One of the city's most famous culinary specialties is the oyster, which is harvested in nearby Thau Lagoon. You can sample these delicious delicacies at one of the many seafood restaurants in Montpellier. For a taste of the local wine, head to one of the city's many wine bars, where you can sample a variety of wines from the Languedoc-Roussillon region.

CONCLUSION

In conclusion, Montpellier is a city with a rich history, a vibrant cultural scene, and a delicious culinary tradition. Whether you're interested in exploring historic architecture, attending a music festival, or indulging in local cuisine, Montpellier has something for everyone. So why not add this charming southern French city to your travel itinerary?

SIBENIK, CROATIA

If you're looking for a hidden gem along the Adriatic coast, look no further than Sibenik. This charming city in Croatia offers a unique blend of history, culture, and natural beauty that's sure to captivate any traveler.

HISTORY

Founded over 1,000 years ago, Sibenik has a rich history that's reflected in its architecture and landmarks. One of its most famous attractions is the UNESCO-listed St. James Cathedral, a stunning example of Renaissance and Gothic styles. Visitors can also explore the historic fortress of St. Michael, which offers panoramic views of the city and surrounding countryside.

CULTURE AND FESTIVALS

Sibenik is also known for its lively cultural scene, with plenty of events and festivals throughout the year. One of the most popular is the International Children's Festival, which takes place in late June and features a range of performances, workshops, and exhibitions for kids of all ages.

NATURAL BEAUTY

Beyond its cultural offerings, Sibenik is surrounded by some of the most beautiful natural scenery in Croatia. The nearby Krka National Park is a must-visit destination, with its cascading waterfalls, hiking trails, and diverse wildlife. Visitors can also take a boat tour to the nearby Kornati Islands, a stunning archipelago of rocky islets and crystal-clear waters.

FINAL THOUGHTS

Whether you're interested in history, culture, or natural beauty, Sibenik offers something for every type of traveler. With its welcoming locals, delicious cuisine, and laid-back atmosphere, it's the perfect destination for a relaxing getaway. So why not add this charming city to your travel itinerary? You won't regret it!

KALMAR, SWEDEN

Kalmar City, located on the southeastern coast of Sweden, is a picturesque destination that is well worth a visit. With a rich history, beautiful architecture, and stunning scenery, Kalmar has something to offer for everyone.

HISTORY AND CULTURE

Kalmar has a long and fascinating history, dating back to the Middle Ages. The city played a crucial role in Swedish politics and was an important center for trade and commerce. Today, visitors can explore Kalmar Castle, which was built in the 12th century and has played a significant role in the city's history.

Another must-visit cultural site is the Kalmar County Museum, which is located in the city center. Here, visitors can learn about the history of the region, including the city's role in the Swedish Reformation, the Kalmar Union, and the Swedish Empire.

ARCHITECTURE

Kalmar is renowned for its beautiful architecture, which is a mix of medieval and modern styles. The city center features a range of historic buildings, including churches, palaces, and townhouses, which have been beautifully preserved.

One of the most iconic buildings in Kalmar is the Kalmar Cathedral, which dates back to the 17th century. The cathedral features stunning Gothic architecture, including a beautiful rose window and ornate altarpieces.

NATURAL BEAUTY

Kalmar is situated on the coast of the Baltic Sea, and the surrounding countryside is characterized by beautiful forests and lakes. The city is also home to several parks and gardens, which provide a peaceful escape from the hustle and bustle of city life.

One of the most popular parks in Kalmar is Stadsparken, which features a beautiful lake, a playground, and several walking trails. Visitors can also take a stroll along the city's waterfront, where they can enjoy stunning views of the sea.

CONCLUSION

In conclusion, Kalmar City is a must-visit destination for anyone traveling to Sweden. With its rich history, beautiful architecture, and stunning natural beauty, it's no wonder that Kalmar is considered one of the jewels of the Swedish east coast. Whether you're interested in history, culture, or simply taking in the sights and sounds of a beautiful city, Kalmar is sure to leave a lasting impression.

SZEGED, HUNGARY

When most people think of traveling to Hungary, Budapest is usually the first city that comes to mind. However, there's a lesser-known city that's definitely worth a visit: Szeged. Located in the southern part of the country, near the border with Serbia, Szeged is the third-largest city in Hungary and is often called the "city of sunshine" because of its warm and sunny weather.

HISTORY AND CULTURE

Szeged has a rich and interesting history that's worth exploring. The city was heavily damaged by a flood in 1879 and had to be almost entirely rebuilt. The rebuilding of the city was influenced by the Art Nouveau style, which is still visible in many of the buildings in the city center. The city also has a strong cultural scene, with many theaters, museums, and galleries. The Szeged Open Air Festival is one of the most popular cultural events in Hungary and takes place every summer.

THINGS TO SEE AND DO

There's no shortage of things to see and do in Szeged. One of the most impressive buildings in the city is the Votive Church, which was built in the early 20th century to give thanks for the city's reconstruction after the flood. The church is an impressive example of Hungarian architecture and has stunning stained glass windows. Another must-see attraction is the Reök Palace, which houses the Ferenc Móra Museum. The museum has an impressive collection of artifacts related to Hungarian history and culture.

FOOD AND DRINK

Hungarian cuisine is famous around the world, and Szeged is no exception. The city has a thriving food and drink scene, with many restaurants, cafes, and bars. One of the most famous dishes in Szeged is the fisherman's soup, which is a spicy soup made with fish and paprika. The city is also known for its wines, especially its white wines. If you're a fan of wine, be sure to visit some of the wineries in the area.

CONCLUSION

Szeged may not be as well-known as Budapest, but it's a city that's definitely worth a visit. With its rich history, impressive architecture, and thriving cultural scene, there's something for everyone in Szeged. And with its warm and sunny weather, it's the perfect destination for a summer vacation.

KRASNOYARSK, RUSSIA

Krasnoyarsk is a city in Russia that is known for its rich history, beautiful natural scenery, and unique culture. It is located in the heart of Siberia and is the third-largest city in the region, after Novosibirsk and Omsk. Whether you are a history buff, an outdoor enthusiast, or just looking for an off-the-beaten-path travel destination, Krasnoyarsk has something to offer.

HISTORY

Krasnoyarsk was founded in 1628 as a Russian fur trading post. It played an important role in the exploration and colonization of Siberia, and was also a center for political exiles and prisoners during the Soviet era. Today, visitors can explore the city's rich history through its many museums and historical sites, such as the Krasnoyarsk Regional Museum and the Vasily Surikov Museum.

NATURE

One of the main attractions of Krasnoyarsk is its stunning natural scenery. The city is located on the banks of the Yenisei River, which is the fifth-longest river in the world. Visitors can take a boat tour or go kayaking on the river, or hike in the nearby Stolby Nature Reserve, which is known for its unique rock formations and breathtaking views.

CULTURE

Krasnoyarsk is also known for its unique culture, which combines elements of traditional Russian culture with influences from the indigenous peoples of Siberia. Visitors can experience this culture through traditional food, music, dance, and art. The city is also home to the Krasnoyarsk Opera and Ballet Theater, which is one of the most prestigious cultural institutions in Russia.

CONCLUSION

Krasnoyarsk may not be the most well-known travel destination in Russia, but it is definitely worth a visit. With its rich history, stunning natural scenery, and unique culture, there is something for everyone in this Siberian city. So why not add Krasnoyarsk to your travel itinerary and discover all that it has to offer?

CORK, IRELAND

Located in the south of Ireland, Cork City is a charming destination that has a lot to offer to travelers. From its rich history to its vibrant nightlife, Cork City is a place that will leave you wanting more. In this article, we will explore some of the highlights of Cork City that make it a must-visit destination for travelers.

HISTORY AND CULTURE

Cork City has a rich history that dates back to the 6th century. The city has been ruled by various powers throughout its history, including the Vikings, the English, and the Irish. This has resulted in a diverse cultural heritage that is evident in the city's architecture, museums, and art galleries. Some of the must-visit historical sites in Cork City include the Cork City Gaol, the English Market, and the Shandon Bells.

FOOD AND DRINK

Cork City is known for its excellent food and drink scene. The English Market is a must-visit for foodies, where you can find everything from fresh seafood to artisanal cheeses. For a taste of the local cuisine, try some traditional Irish dishes like Irish stew or fish and chips. The city is also home to a thriving craft beer scene, with a range of microbreweries and pubs serving up unique and delicious beers.

OUTDOOR ACTIVITIES

Cork City is surrounded by beautiful countryside, making it an ideal destination for outdoor enthusiasts. Take a stroll through Fitzgerald Park or explore the Cork City Walks to get a taste of the natural beauty that the city has to offer. For those looking for more adventure, try kayaking on the River Lee or hiking in the nearby mountains.

NIGHTLIFE

Cork City is known for its vibrant nightlife, with a range of bars, pubs, and nightclubs to suit all tastes. Whether you're looking for a quiet pint in a traditional Irish pub or a night of dancing in a trendy nightclub, Cork City has something to offer. The city also hosts a range of festivals and events throughout the year, including the Cork Jazz Festival and the Cork Midsummer Festival.

CONCLUSION

Cork City is a charming destination that offers something for everyone. With its rich history, excellent food and drink scene, outdoor activities, and vibrant nightlife, Cork City is a must-visit destination for travelers. So, pack your bags and head to Cork City for an unforgettable experience!

RETHYMNO, GREECE

Rethymno City is a beautiful coastal town located in the island of Crete, Greece. The city is rich in history, culture, and natural beauty, making it a perfect destination for travelers who want to experience the Greek island life.

OLD TOWN

The Old Town of Rethymno is a maze of narrow streets, alleys, and Venetian-style buildings. It's a perfect place to wander around and get lost in the beautiful architecture and history of the city. You can also visit the Rimondi Fountain, the Fortezza castle, and the beautiful Venetian Harbor.

BEACHES

The city boasts some of the most beautiful beaches in Greece. The most popular beaches include the Rethymno Beach, the Ammoudi Beach, and the Gerani Beach. These beaches offer crystal clear waters, soft sand, and stunning views of the surrounding mountains and coastline.

LOCAL CUISINE

The local cuisine in Rethymno City is a fusion of Greek, Turkish, and Venetian influences. The city is famous for its delicious seafood, fresh vegetables, and local wines. You can find many restaurants and taverns in the Old

Town and along the beachfront where you can taste the local delicacies.

FESTIVALS

Rethymno City is known for its lively festivals and cultural events. The most popular festivals include the Renaissance Festival in July, the Wine Festival in August, and the Cretan Diet Festival in September. These festivals offer a unique opportunity to experience the local culture and traditions.

CONCLUSION

Rethymno City is a perfect destination for travelers who want to experience the beauty and culture of Greece. Whether you want to explore the Old Town, relax on the beaches, taste the local cuisine, or take part in the festivals, Rethymno City has something for everyone. Book your trip now and enjoy a memorable vacation in this stunning city.

VIANDEN, LUXEMBOURG

Vianden is a small city located in the north of Luxembourg, close to the border with Germany. It is a popular destination for travelers seeking a peaceful and picturesque retreat. The city is known for its well-preserved medieval architecture, stunning natural scenery, and rich cultural heritage.

GETTING THERE

Vianden is easily accessible by car or public transport. The closest airport is Luxembourg Airport, which is approximately 50 km away. From the airport, visitors can take a bus or taxi to Vianden. It is also possible to reach the city by train or bus from Luxembourg City, which is about 45 km away.

EXPLORING THE CITY

One of the main attractions in Vianden is the impressive Vianden Castle, which dates back to the 11th century. The castle is perched on a hill overlooking the city and offers stunning views of the surrounding landscape. Visitors can explore the castle and its museum, which showcases the history and culture of the region.

Another popular attraction in Vianden is the Victor Hugo House, the former home of the famous French writer. The house has been converted into a museum and offers a glimpse into the life and works of the author.

For those interested in nature, the city also offers several hiking trails through the picturesque Ardennes forest. Visitors can also take a scenic chairlift ride to the top of the hill to enjoy panoramic views of the city and the surrounding countryside.

CULTURE AND CUISINE

Vianden is known for its rich cultural heritage, which is reflected in the city's museums, art galleries, and festivals. The city hosts several cultural events throughout the year, including the International Festival of Street Theater and the medieval festival.

The city also boasts a vibrant culinary scene, with a variety of restaurants and cafes serving traditional Luxembourgish cuisine, as well as international dishes. Local specialties include Judd mat Gaardebounen (smoked pork neck with broad beans) and Bouneschlupp (a hearty bean soup).

ACCOMMODATION

Vianden offers a range of accommodation options, including hotels, guesthouses, and campsites. Visitors can choose from charming historic hotels in the city center or more modern accommodations with scenic views of the surrounding countryside.

CONCLUSION

Vianden is a charming medieval city that offers visitors a perfect blend of natural beauty, rich cultural heritage, and delicious cuisine. Whether you are interested in history, nature, or simply a relaxing getaway, Vianden is a must-visit destination in Luxembourg.

JÖNKÖPING, SWEDEN

Jönköping City, located in the southern part of Sweden, is a beautiful and vibrant city that is worth visiting. It is situated on the shores of the Vättern, Sweden's second-largest lake, and offers a mix of nature, culture, and modern amenities.

LOCATION AND GETTING THERE

Jönköping City is located in the Småland region of Sweden and is easily accessible by car or public transportation. The city is located on the E4 highway, which connects Stockholm and Malmö. There is also a train station in the city center that offers connections to major cities in Sweden.

THINGS TO DO

Jönköping City offers a range of activities for visitors. Nature lovers can explore the beautiful Vättern Lake, which offers opportunities for swimming, boating, and fishing. The city also has several parks and nature reserves, including the scenic Huskvarna Falls.

Culture enthusiasts can visit the Jönköping County Museum, which showcases the history and culture of the region. The city is also home to several galleries and theaters that feature contemporary art and performances.

For shoppers, Jönköping City offers a mix of international brands and local boutiques. The city center is pedestrian-friendly and offers a variety of shops, cafes, and restaurants.

ACCOMMODATION AND DINING

Jönköping City offers a range of accommodation options, from budget-friendly hostels to luxury hotels. Many of the hotels are located in the city center and offer easy access to the city's attractions.

The city's dining scene offers a mix of traditional Swedish cuisine and international flavors. Visitors can enjoy everything from classic Swedish meatballs to sushi and pizza.

CONCLUSION

Overall, Jönköping City is a destination worth visiting for anyone traveling to Sweden. With its mix of nature, culture, and modern amenities, there is something for everyone in this beautiful and vibrant city.

PIRAN, SLOVENIA

Slovenia is a small country situated in central Europe, and it is known for its natural beauty, cultural heritage, and hospitable locals. Piran, a coastal city situated on the Adriatic Sea, is one of the most popular tourist destinations in Slovenia. The city has a rich history, and its architecture reflects a unique blend of Venetian and Slovenian styles.

LOCATION AND GETTING THERE

Piran is located on the southwestern coast of Slovenia, close to the border with Italy and Croatia. The city is easily accessible by car, bus, or train from nearby cities such as Ljubljana and Trieste. Visitors can also fly into the nearby airports of Ljubljana or Trieste and then take a bus or car to Piran.

THINGS TO DO

Piran is a small city, but it has a lot to offer to tourists. The city's main attraction is the old town, which is situated on a small peninsula and is surrounded by the sea. The old town is home to several historical buildings, churches, and museums, including the Tartini Museum, which is dedicated to the famous violinist and composer, Giuseppe Tartini.

Visitors can also take a walk along the city's promenade, which offers stunning views of the sea and the surrounding hills. The promenade is also a great place to relax and enjoy the local cuisine, which includes fresh seafood, olive oil, and local wines.

Another popular attraction in Piran is the city's beaches. The city has several beaches, including the popular Portoroz Beach, which is located just a few kilometers from the city center. Visitors can enjoy swimming, sunbathing, and other water sports activities in the crystal clear waters of the Adriatic Sea.

ACCOMMODATIONS AND DINING

Piran has a range of accommodation options to suit all budgets, from luxury hotels to budget hostels. Visitors can also choose to stay in one of the many private apartments or villas that are available for rent. As for dining, Piran offers a range of restaurants and cafes, serving local and international cuisine.

CONCLUSION

Piran is a hidden gem on the Slovenian coast, and it is a must-visit destination for anyone who loves history, culture, and natural beauty. The city's old town, beaches, and cuisine offer something for everyone, and its hospitable locals will make you feel right at home. So, if you're planning a trip to Slovenia, be sure to add Piran to your itinerary.

SOLOTHURN, SWITZERLAND

Nestled along the Aare River, Solothurn is a picturesque town located in the north-west of Switzerland. With its charming Old Town, breathtaking architecture, and rich cultural heritage, this city has plenty to offer for travelers seeking a relaxing and memorable experience.

HISTORY AND CULTURE

Solothurn boasts a rich history dating back to Roman times. The town has a range of historical landmarks, including the impressive St. Ursen Cathedral, which was built in the late 18th century. Visitors can also explore the Old Town and its many museums, such as the Kunstmuseum Solothurn and the Naturmuseum Solothurn, which showcase the city's rich cultural heritage.

ARCHITECTURE

The city's architecture is a blend of various styles, from Baroque to Art Nouveau. One of the most striking buildings in Solothurn is the imposing St. Ursen Gate, which is one of the few remaining city gates in Switzerland. Other notable buildings include the impressive Jesuit Church, the Rathaus (Town Hall), and the Solothurner Zeughaus (Armory).

LEISURE AND RECREATION

For those seeking outdoor recreation, Solothurn has plenty to offer. The nearby Jura Mountains provide a stunning backdrop for hiking and cycling. The Aare River is perfect for kayaking and rafting, and there are plenty of swimming spots along its banks.

CUISINE

Solothurn is also a haven for foodies, with a range of restaurants and cafes serving up delicious Swiss cuisine. From traditional Swiss cheese fondue to exquisite chocolate, visitors can indulge in a variety of mouth-watering delicacies.

CONCLUSION

Solothurn is a hidden gem in Switzerland that offers visitors a blend of history, culture, architecture, and outdoor recreation. Whether you're looking to explore the city's rich cultural heritage, indulge in Swiss cuisine, or simply soak up the stunning natural scenery, Solothurn is a must-visit destination for anyone traveling to Switzerland.

GDANSK, POLAND

Gdansk is a beautiful and historic city located on the coast of the Baltic Sea in northern Poland. The city is known for its rich history, stunning architecture, and vibrant cultural scene.

HISTORY

Gdansk has a long and fascinating history that dates back to the 10th century. The city has been shaped by various rulers and empires over the years, including the Teutonic Knights, the Polish-Lithuanian Commonwealth, and the German Empire. The city played a crucial role in the outbreak of World War II, and it was heavily damaged during the war. However, it has been meticulously restored to its former glory in recent years.

ARCHITECTURE

Gdansk boasts a stunning array of architecture that reflects the city's rich history. Visitors can explore the medieval Old Town, which features Gothic and Renaissance buildings, charming narrow streets, and picturesque squares. The city is also home to numerous historic churches, including St. Mary's Church, which is the largest brick church in the world.

CULTURE

Gdansk has a vibrant cultural scene that includes museums, galleries, theaters, and music venues. The city is particularly renowned for its amber, which has been mined in the Baltic region for centuries. Visitors can learn about amber at the Amber Museum, which features a vast collection of amber jewelry and artifacts.

CONCLUSION

Gdansk is a stunning city that offers visitors a fascinating glimpse into Poland's rich history and culture. With its beautiful architecture, vibrant cultural scene, and scenic location on the Baltic Sea, it's no wonder that Gdansk is becoming an increasingly popular destination for travelers from around the world.

VENTSPILS, LATVIA

Ventspils is a charming coastal city located in the northwestern region of Latvia, facing the Baltic Sea. With a population of around 40,000 inhabitants, it is the sixth-largest city in the country and serves as a major hub for trade and tourism.

HISTORY

The city of Ventspils has a long and storied history dating back to the 13th century. Originally a small fishing village, it quickly grew into an important center for trade, commerce, and shipping. Throughout the centuries, it has been ruled by various powers, including the Livonian Order, the Polish-Lithuanian Commonwealth, and the Russian Empire.

TOURISM

Today, Ventspils is known as a popular tourist destination, thanks in part to its beautiful coastline and rich cultural heritage. Visitors can explore the town's historic Old Town district, which features numerous examples of traditional Latvian architecture. They can also visit the Ventspils Museum, which showcases the city's fascinating history, as well as the Seaside Open-Air Museum, which offers a glimpse into the life of a 19th-century fishing village.

In addition, Ventspils is home to a wide range of outdoor activities, including sailing, windsurfing, and cycling. The town's stunning beach is perfect for swimming and sunbathing, while the nearby forests and nature trails offer endless opportunities for hiking and exploring.

INFRASTRUCTURE

Ventspils boasts excellent infrastructure, including modern hotels, restaurants, and shops. The city also has a well-developed transportation network, with regular bus and train services connecting it to other major cities in Latvia and beyond.

CONCLUSION

In conclusion, Ventspils is a hidden gem that is well worth a visit for anyone traveling to Latvia. With its beautiful coastline, rich history, and range of outdoor activities, it has something to offer everyone. So why not add it to your itinerary and experience the magic of this charming seaside town for yourself?

ERFURT, GERMANY

Erfurt is a beautiful city located in the heart of Germany, with a rich history and a vibrant culture. It is the capital of the state of Thuringia, known for its stunning architecture, picturesque landscapes, and warm hospitality.

DISCOVERING THE OLD TOWN

The city's Old Town is a must-see attraction for visitors, with its narrow streets, medieval buildings, and charming atmosphere. The iconic Erfurt Cathedral, St. Mary's Church, and the impressive Krämerbrücke (Merchant's Bridge) are just some of the landmarks that await you.

CULTURAL HOTSPOTS

Erfurt is home to numerous museums and cultural institutions, such as the Angermuseum, the Thüringer Landesmuseum, and the Bauhaus Museum. The city is also famous for its theater scene, with the Theater Erfurt and the Deutsche Nationaltheater among the most popular venues.

A CULINARY DELIGHT

Erfurt's culinary scene is a treat for foodies, with a variety of local specialties that will satisfy any palate. Thüringer Rostbratwurst, a type of sausage, is a must-try dish, as well as the famous Eierschecke, a traditional cake made with eggs and quark cheese.

NATURE AND OUTDOOR ACTIVITIES

Surrounded by forests and hills, Erfurt is the perfect destination for nature lovers and outdoor enthusiasts. The Gera River and the nearby Thuringian Forest offer a wide range of activities, such as hiking, cycling, and canoeing.

GETTING AROUND

Erfurt is easily accessible by train or car, and the city has an efficient public transportation system. Walking is also a great way to explore the city's many sights, as most attractions are located within walking distance from each other.

FINAL THOUGHTS

Erfurt is a hidden gem in Germany, waiting to be discovered by travelers. With its rich cultural heritage, stunning architecture, and scenic surroundings, it is a perfect destination for a weekend getaway or a longer vacation.

AVEIRO, PORTUGAL

Aveiro is a charming coastal city located in the central region of Portugal. Known as the "Venice of Portugal," Aveiro is famous for its picturesque canals, colorful moliceiro boats, and stunning Art Nouveau architecture.

EXPLORING THE CANALS

One of the best ways to experience Aveiro's beauty is by taking a ride on a moliceiro boat, which takes you through the city's canals. These boats were once used for seaweed harvesting and transportation but are now a popular tourist attraction. During the ride, you can admire the city's colorful buildings, bridges, and scenic views of the Ria de Aveiro lagoon.

ART AND ARCHITECTURE

Aveiro is home to several stunning Art Nouveau buildings, including the Aveiro Museum, the São João Evangelista Chapel, and the Aveiro Train Station. The buildings feature intricate details, colorful tiles, and unique designs that make them stand out.

BEACHES AND PARKS

Aveiro is not only known for its city charm, but it also boasts some beautiful beaches and parks. The Costa Nova Beach is famous for its striped houses and clean sands, while the Barra Beach is known for its waves and surfing. The city also has several parks, including the João Paulo II Park, which offers a peaceful escape from the hustle and bustle of the city.

GASTRONOMY

Aveiro is also a great destination for foodies. The city is known for its delicious seafood, including octopus, squid, and sardines. The traditional "ovos moles," a sweet pastry made of egg yolks and sugar, is also a must-try dessert.

IN CONCLUSION

Aveiro is a unique destination that offers a perfect blend of natural beauty, rich culture, and delicious cuisine. Whether you are looking for a relaxing getaway or an exciting adventure, Aveiro has something for everyone.

LECCE, ITALY

If you're looking for a destination in Southern Italy that's off the beaten path, consider Lecce. Known as the "Florence of the South," this small city is a treasure trove of Baroque architecture, historic landmarks, and delicious food.

HISTORY AND CULTURE

Lecce has a rich history dating back to the ancient Roman times, but it's the Baroque era that left the most significant mark on the city. The ornate buildings, churches, and piazzas are a testament to the Baroque style that dominated Southern Italy in the 17th and 18th centuries.

The city is also known for its papier-mâché art, which you can see on display at the Museo della Cartapesta. If you're interested in learning more about the local culture, visit the Pinacoteca di Palazzo dei Celestini, which houses an impressive collection of paintings from the 14th to 18th centuries.

ARCHITECTURE AND LANDMARKS

Lecce's historic center is a UNESCO World Heritage Site, and it's easy to see why. The intricate facades, columns, and statues of the buildings are a sight to behold. Some of the must-see landmarks include the Basilica di Santa Croce, Piazza del Duomo, and the Roman Amphitheater.

FOOD AND DRINK

Like all Italian cities, Lecce has plenty of delicious food and wine to enjoy. The local cuisine features fresh seafood, handmade pasta, and plenty of olive oil. Don't miss the chance to try the local specialty, pasticciotto, a custard-filled pastry that's perfect for breakfast or dessert.

CONCLUSION

Lecce may not be as well-known as some of Italy's larger cities, but it's a hidden gem that's worth exploring. Whether you're interested in history, architecture, or just delicious food, there's something for everyone in this charming Baroque city.

DELFT, NETHERLANDS

Delft is a charming city in the Netherlands, known for its picturesque canals, historic architecture, and cultural significance. The city has a rich history, dating back to the 13th century, and is famous for being the birthplace of the famous Dutch painter, Johannes Vermeer. With its quaint streets, cozy cafes, and numerous cultural attractions, Delft is a must-visit destination for anyone exploring the Netherlands.

GETTING TO DELFT

Delft is conveniently located between Rotterdam and The Hague, and can be easily reached by train, bus, or car. The closest airport is Rotterdam The Hague Airport, which is just a 20-minute drive away. From Amsterdam, it takes about an hour to reach Delft by train, and the journey is both scenic and comfortable.

EXPLORING DELFT

One of the best ways to explore Delft is by foot or bicycle. The city is small and easy to navigate, with numerous landmarks and attractions located within walking distance. Visitors can stroll along the charming canals, admire the historic buildings and churches, and visit the famous Delftware factories.

CULTURAL ATTRACTIONS

Delft is a city rich in cultural attractions, with numerous museums, galleries, and historic sites. The Vermeer Centrum Delft is a must-visit for art enthusiasts, showcasing the life and works of the famous painter Johannes Vermeer. Other notable museums include the Museum Prinsenhof Delft, which explores the history of the Dutch royal family, and the Science Centre Delft, which showcases cutting-edge scientific research.

DINING AND NIGHTLIFE

Delft is home to numerous cozy cafes, trendy bars, and restaurants serving up delicious Dutch cuisine. Visitors can sample traditional Dutch snacks, such as stroopwafels and bitterballen, or enjoy a meal at one of the city's many restaurants serving up local specialties. The city also has a vibrant nightlife scene, with numerous bars and clubs catering to a variety of tastes.

CONCLUSION

Delft is a charming city that is well worth a visit for anyone exploring the Netherlands. With its picturesque canals, historic architecture, and cultural attractions, the city has something for everyone. Whether you're interested in art, history, or simply soaking up the local culture, Delft is a destination that is sure to leave a lasting impression.

BLED, SLOVENIA

Nestled in the foothills of the Julian Alps, Bled is a quaint and charming town located in northwestern Slovenia. It is a popular tourist destination known for its breathtaking natural beauty, rich cultural heritage, and plethora of outdoor activities. Here is a glimpse into what this picturesque city has to offer.

THE NATURAL BEAUTY OF BLED

Bled is famous for its stunning natural landscape, particularly Lake Bled. The lake is surrounded by lush forests, rolling hills, and towering mountains, making it a popular destination for nature enthusiasts. Visitors can take a leisurely walk around the lake, rent a boat to explore its crystal-clear waters, or even swim in its pristine waters during the warmer months.

CULTURE AND HISTORY

Bled is also rich in culture and history, with a long-standing tradition of hospitality and warm welcome to visitors. The town is home to several historic landmarks, including the iconic Bled Castle, which sits atop a hill overlooking the town and lake. The castle dates back to the 11th century and offers visitors a glimpse into the area's medieval past.

OUTDOOR ACTIVITIES

Bled is a haven for outdoor enthusiasts, with plenty of activities to suit all interests and skill levels. Hiking and mountain biking are popular pursuits, with numerous trails winding through the surrounding mountains. The town also has a thriving water sports scene, with kayaking, canoeing, and paddleboarding among the most popular activities.

CULINARY DELIGHTS

Finally, no trip to Bled is complete without sampling some of the region's culinary delights. The town is known for its delicious local cuisine, with traditional dishes such as kremna rezina (cream cake) and blejska kremna rezina (Bled cream cake) being popular favorites. Visitors can also enjoy locally produced wines and spirits, such as the region's signature brandy, known as borovniček.

IN CONCLUSION

Bled is a truly special destination that offers something for everyone. Whether you're looking for outdoor adventure, cultural experiences, or just a relaxing getaway surrounded by breathtaking natural beauty, Bled is sure to delight.

OBAN, SCOTLAND

Nestled on the west coast of Scotland, Oban is a picturesque town that serves as the gateway to the Scottish Isles. With a population of just over 8,000 people, Oban has a charm and character that draws visitors from all over the world. Here's what you need to know about this Scottish gem.

LOCATION AND ACCESSIBILITY

Oban is located on the coast of Argyll and Bute, about 90 miles northwest of Glasgow. It's easily accessible by car, bus, or train, making it a popular destination for both locals and tourists. The town also has a small airport that offers flights to the Scottish islands.

THINGS TO DO

Oban is known for its seafood, and visitors can enjoy fresh seafood at one of the many restaurants in town. The Oban Distillery is another popular attraction, where visitors can learn about the history of whiskey-making in Scotland and sample some of the local brews. There are also several historic sites in and around Oban, including Dunollie Castle and the McCaig's Tower.

ISLAND HOPPING

One of the biggest draws of Oban is its proximity to the Scottish Isles. Visitors can take a ferry from Oban to several different islands, including Mull, Iona, and Staffa. Each island has its own unique attractions, from the stunning beaches of Mull to the mysterious Fingal's Cave on Staffa.

ACCOMMODATION

Oban has a range of accommodation options, from budget hostels to luxury hotels. Many visitors choose to stay in one of the town's charming bed and breakfasts, which offer a cozy and authentic Scottish experience.

FINAL THOUGHTS

Whether you're looking to explore the Scottish Isles or simply relax in a quaint coastal town, Oban has something to offer. With its stunning scenery, rich history, and friendly locals, it's no wonder that Oban is a popular destination for travelers from around the world.

LEÓN, SPAIN

León is a picturesque city located in the northwest of Spain and is the capital of the León province. The city boasts of its rich history and culture, making it an ideal destination for travelers who love to immerse themselves in the local culture.

THE HISTORIC QUARTER

The Historic Quarter of León is considered a living museum and is one of the most well-preserved medieval quarters in Europe. The quarter features several ancient landmarks, such as the Gothic-style Cathedral of León, which is one of the most famous attractions in the city. The cathedral is known for its stunning stained glass windows, and it also houses a museum where visitors can learn about the history of the city.

CULTURE AND TRADITION

León is also known for its vibrant cultural scene, with several art museums and galleries showcasing the works of local artists. The city is also home to many traditional festivals and celebrations, such as the Semana Santa (Holy Week) and the San Juan y San Pedro Festival, which are popular among both locals and tourists.

GASTRONOMY

The gastronomy of León is influenced by the Castile and León region, and the city is known for its traditional dishes, such as cocido maragato, which is a hearty stew made with meat and vegetables. The city is also famous for its cured meats, such as chorizo and salchichón, and its cheeses, such as queso de Valdeón, which is a blue cheese made from cow and goat milk.

NATURE AND ADVENTURE

León is also an ideal destination for nature lovers and adventure enthusiasts. The city is located near the Picos de Europa National Park, which is a popular destination for hiking and climbing. The park features several hiking trails, including the Ruta del Cares, which is a popular trail that offers stunning views of the surrounding mountains.

IN CONCLUSION

León is a hidden gem in the Castile and León region, offering visitors a unique blend of history, culture, gastronomy, and adventure. It is an ideal destination for those who want to immerse themselves in the local culture and experience the beauty of nature.

CHANIA, GREECE

Chania is a beautiful coastal city located on the island of Crete, Greece. It is a hidden gem that is not as well-known as some of the other tourist destinations in Greece, making it a perfect place for those seeking a more peaceful and authentic Greek experience.

HISTORY AND CULTURE

Chania has a rich history and culture dating back to the Minoan civilization. It was ruled by various empires, including the Venetians and Ottomans, which has influenced its architecture, cuisine, and customs. The city is filled with historical landmarks, such as the Venetian Harbor, the Ottoman-era mosque and church, and the Archaeological Museum of Chania.

FOOD AND DRINK

Greek cuisine is famous worldwide, and Chania offers some of the best dishes on the island of Crete. You can find traditional tavernas that serve mouth-watering dishes made from fresh local ingredients. Try some of the local specialties, such as Dakos, Kalitsounia, and Sfakiani Pita. Don't forget to pair your meal with a glass of Cretan wine or raki, a local spirit.

BEACHES AND NATURE

Chania is blessed with beautiful beaches and breathtaking landscapes. Balos and Elafonissi beaches are some of the most popular and picturesque beaches in Chania. Samaria Gorge is a must-visit for nature lovers, offering a stunning hiking trail that takes you through the gorge, where you can see rare flora and fauna.

NIGHTLIFE

Chania's nightlife is not as wild as some of the other Greek islands, but it still offers plenty of options for those looking for a good time. There are many bars and clubs that cater to different tastes and preferences, from cozy pubs to lively nightclubs.

IN CONCLUSION

Chania, Greece, is a hidden gem that offers a perfect blend of history, culture, food, nature, and nightlife. Whether you're a history buff, a foodie, or a nature lover, there's something for everyone in Chania. So pack your bags and explore this beautiful city on your next trip to Greece.

KARLOVY VARY, CZECH REPUBLIC

Karlovy Vary, also known as Carlsbad, is a beautiful city located in the western part of the Czech Republic. This stunning destination is renowned for its natural hot springs and is considered to be the spa capital of the country.

A RICH HISTORY

Karlovy Vary has a rich history dating back to the 14th century. The city was named after King Charles IV, who founded the city and discovered its thermal springs. Over the years, the city has attracted numerous famous personalities including Beethoven, Goethe, and Freud, who all came to experience the healing powers of the natural hot springs.

STUNNING ARCHITECTURE

Karlovy Vary is a picturesque city with stunning architecture that is sure to take your breath away. The city is home to numerous spa buildings that were built during the 19th century, which have been preserved to this day. The buildings are a testament to the city's rich history and provide an insight into the past.

NATURAL HOT SPRINGS

One of the biggest attractions of Karlovy Vary is its natural hot springs. The city is home to numerous thermal springs that are rich in minerals and have healing properties. The springs are believed to help with various ailments, including digestive problems, arthritis, and skin conditions.

INTERNATIONAL FILM FESTIVAL

Karlovy Vary is also known for hosting the annual International Film Festival. This prestigious event attracts filmmakers, actors, and movie enthusiasts from all over the world. The festival showcases some of the best films from different genres and provides a platform for emerging filmmakers.

FINAL THOUGHTS

Karlovy Vary is a stunning destination that should be on every traveler's bucket list. The city's rich history, stunning architecture, natural hot springs, and cultural events make it an unforgettable experience. Whether you're looking to relax and unwind or explore a new culture, Karlovy Vary has something for everyone.

KILKENNY, IRELAND

Kilkenny City, located in the heart of Ireland's Ancient East, is a charming and vibrant town that attracts visitors from all over the world. Steeped in history and culture, Kilkenny is a must-see destination for anyone interested in Irish heritage and tradition.

HISTORY AND CULTURE

Kilkenny has a rich and fascinating history that dates back over 800 years. The city is home to many historical landmarks, including the magnificent Kilkenny Castle, which was built in the 12th century and is now open to the public. Visitors can also explore the Medieval Mile, a walk through the heart of the city's medieval past that includes St. Canice's Cathedral, Rothe House, and the Black Abbey.

FOOD AND DRINK

Kilkenny is a food lover's paradise, with a wide variety of restaurants, cafes, and pubs serving delicious local cuisine. Visitors can sample traditional Irish dishes like shepherd's pie, fish and chips, and Irish stew, as well as more modern fare like sushi and tapas. The city is also famous for its beer, with the Smithwick's Brewery located right in the heart of town.

SHOPPING

Kilkenny is a great place to shop, with a mix of high-end boutiques, independent stores, and traditional Irish craft shops. Visitors can browse for unique souvenirs like handmade pottery, jewelry, and textiles, or shop for designer fashion and accessories.

ENTERTAINMENT

Kilkenny is known for its lively entertainment scene, with a wide range of music, theater, and comedy performances taking place throughout the year. The city is home to many music venues, including the Set Theatre and the Kilkenny Tradfest, an annual festival celebrating traditional Irish music.

OUTDOOR ACTIVITIES

For those who love the outdoors, Kilkenny offers a range of activities, including hiking, fishing, and golf. The city is surrounded by beautiful countryside, with the River Nore running through the heart of town.

CONCLUSION

Kilkenny City is a must-visit destination for anyone traveling to Ireland. With its rich history, delicious cuisine, great shopping, and lively entertainment scene, there is something for everyone in this charming and vibrant town. So come and experience the beauty and culture of Kilkenny for yourself!

FUNCHAL, PORTUGAL

Funchal, the capital of Portugal's Madeira archipelago, is a charming and picturesque city located on the southern coast of the island. The city is known for its mild climate, beautiful beaches, historic architecture, and stunning natural scenery, making it a popular destination for tourists from all over the world.

HISTORIC DISTRICT

Funchal's historic district is a must-visit for anyone interested in architecture and history. Here, visitors can see buildings from the 15th to the 19th centuries, such as the Cathedral of Funchal, the Church of São Pedro, and the Fort of São Tiago. The district also has several museums, including the Madeira Wine Museum and the Contemporary Art Museum, that showcase the region's history and culture.

BEACHES

Funchal has several beaches where visitors can relax and soak up the sun. Praia Formosa is the largest and most popular beach in the city, offering stunning views of the Atlantic Ocean and plenty of activities, including surfing, paddleboarding, and kayaking. Other beaches in Funchal include Praia do Gorgulho and Praia dos Reis Magos, both of which are perfect for swimming and sunbathing.

NATURAL BEAUTY

Funchal is surrounded by stunning natural scenery, making it a great destination for nature lovers. Visitors can take a cable car ride to the Monte Palace Tropical Garden, which features exotic plants and stunning views of the city. The Madeira Botanical Garden is another popular attraction, showcasing over 2,000 species of plants from around the world.

CULINARY DELIGHTS

Funchal is known for its delicious food and drink, with several restaurants and bars offering traditional Madeiran cuisine and wine. Some of the most popular dishes in Funchal include Espetada (grilled meat skewers), Bolo do Caco (a type of bread), and Poncha (a traditional alcoholic beverage made with honey, lemon, and aguardente).

IN CONCLUSION

Funchal is a wonderful destination that offers something for everyone, from history and culture to natural beauty and delicious food. Whether you're interested in exploring the city's historic district, relaxing on its beaches, or enjoying its culinary delights, Funchal is sure to provide a memorable experience.

VLADIVOSTOK, RUSSIA

Nestled on the eastern coast of Russia lies Vladivostok, a port city that serves as the gateway to the Pacific Ocean. With a population of just over 600,000, Vladivostok is the largest city in the Russian Far East and one of the most important economic and cultural centers in the region.

THE CITYSCAPE

Vladivostok boasts an eclectic mix of architecture, with influences ranging from Russian and Soviet to Chinese, Korean, and Japanese. The city's skyline is dominated by the impressive suspension bridge that spans the Golden Horn Bay, one of the city's most iconic landmarks. Visitors can also explore the historic district, which features well-preserved examples of 19th and early 20th-century buildings.

THINGS TO DO

Vladivostok offers plenty of attractions for visitors of all ages. The city's top tourist destination is the Vladivostok Fortress Museum, which showcases the military history of the region. Other popular sites include the Arsenyev Regional History Museum, the Submarine Museum, and the Botanical Garden. For outdoor enthusiasts, there are several parks and hiking trails that offer breathtaking views of the city and its surroundings.

FOOD AND DRINK

Vladivostok is known for its seafood, and visitors should not miss the chance to try fresh crab, shrimp, and salmon. The city also has a vibrant nightlife scene, with numerous bars, clubs, and restaurants offering a range of international and local cuisine.

GETTING THERE

Vladivostok is easily accessible by air, with direct flights from Moscow, Beijing, Seoul, and other major cities. The city also has a busy port, and several ferries operate between Vladivostok and Japan, South Korea, and China.

CONCLUSION

Vladivostok is a city with a rich history and a vibrant cultural scene. From its stunning architecture and museums to its delicious cuisine and natural beauty, there is something for everyone in this gateway to the Pacific. Whether you are a first-time visitor or a seasoned traveler, Vladivostok is a destination that should not be missed.

ADANA, TURKEY

Adana, located in the south-central part of Turkey, is a city steeped in history and culture. With a population of over 1.7 million people, it is the fifth largest city in Turkey and a popular destination for both domestic and international tourists.

HISTORY AND CULTURE

Adana has a rich history dating back to the Hittites in the 16th century BC. The city has been ruled by various civilizations, including the Persians, Greeks, Romans, Byzantines, and Ottomans, all of whom have left their mark on the city's architecture and culture. Today, Adana is known for its traditional Turkish cuisine, which features local specialties such as kebab and künefe.

ATTRACTIONS

One of the most popular attractions in Adana is the Sabanci Merkez Mosque, a stunning modern mosque that can accommodate over 28,000 worshipers. Another must-see attraction is the Adana Archaeological Museum, which houses a vast collection of artifacts from the Hittite, Roman, and Byzantine periods.

For those interested in outdoor activities, Adana offers many parks and natural attractions, including the Seyhan Dam and the Yumurtalik Nature Reserve. Visitors can also take a boat tour of the Seyhan River or visit the historic stone bridge, Taşköprü.

SHOPPING

Adana is home to many traditional bazaars and markets where visitors can purchase local handicrafts, spices, and textiles. The most famous of these is the Grand Bazaar, which is located in the heart of the city and offers a wide variety of goods.

CONCLUSION

Adana is a vibrant city with a rich history and culture, offering visitors a unique blend of ancient and modern experiences. Whether you're interested in history, culture, cuisine, or outdoor activities, Adana has something for everyone. So, if you're planning a trip to Turkey, be sure to add Adana to your itinerary!

GRONAU, GERMANY

Gronau is a charming city located in the northwestern part of Germany, close to the Dutch border. With a population of just over 47,000 people, Gronau is a relatively small city that has a lot to offer to tourists who are looking for a unique travel experience.

CULTURE AND HISTORY

One of the main attractions in Gronau is the Rock'n'Pop-museum, which showcases the rich musical history of the region. Visitors can explore the exhibits and learn about the famous musicians who have lived and worked in the area.

The city also has a rich cultural history, and tourists can explore landmarks such as the Stadtpark and the Heimatmuseum, which provide insights into the local culture and traditions.

NATURE AND OUTDOOR ACTIVITIES

Gronau is surrounded by beautiful natural landscapes, making it an ideal destination for outdoor enthusiasts. The Dreiländersee is a popular lake that offers opportunities for swimming, boating, and fishing.

The city is also home to several parks and nature reserves, such as the Amtsvenn Nature Park and the Hof Schulte-Günne Park, which are great places for hiking, biking, and birdwatching.

SHOPPING AND DINING

Gronau has a vibrant shopping scene, with several local boutiques and markets offering unique goods and souvenirs. The city also has a variety of dining options, ranging from traditional German cuisine to international fare.

CONCLUSION

Overall, Gronau is a hidden gem in Germany that offers something for everyone. Whether you are interested in history, culture, nature, or simply relaxing, this charming city is definitely worth a visit.

RIJEKA, CROATIA

Located on the Adriatic coast of Croatia, Rijeka is a vibrant city with a rich history and diverse culture. Despite being the third-largest city in Croatia, it often gets overshadowed by the more popular destinations of Dubrovnik, Split, and Zagreb. However, those who take the time to visit Rijeka will be rewarded with a unique and authentic travel experience.

GETTING TO RIJEKA

Rijeka is easily accessible by plane, train, or car. The closest airport is Rijeka Airport, which is located on the nearby island of Krk. The city also has a train station and a bus station, making it easy to arrive from other parts of Croatia or neighboring countries.

EXPLORING THE CITY

Rijeka's historic center is a maze of narrow streets, colorful buildings, and charming squares. Start your exploration at Korzo, the city's main pedestrian street, and wander through the Old Town, where you'll find landmarks like the City Tower, the Cathedral of St. Vitus, and the Governor's Palace.

The city is also home to several interesting museums, including the Maritime and History Museum of the Croatian Littoral, the Peek&Poke Computer Museum, and the Museum of Modern and Contemporary Art.

FOOD AND DRINK

Croatian cuisine is a mix of Mediterranean and Eastern European influences, and Rijeka's restaurants serve up some of the best local dishes. Try the seafood, which is always fresh and flavorful, or sample some of the traditional meat dishes like čevapčići (grilled minced meat), sarma (stuffed cabbage rolls), and ćevapčići (spicy sausage). Wash it all down with a glass of local wine or rakija, a potent fruit brandy that's popular throughout the region.

EVENTS AND FESTIVALS

Rijeka is known for its lively cultural scene and hosts a variety of events and festivals throughout the year. The Rijeka Carnival, held in February or March, is one of the city's most popular events and features colorful parades, street performances, and music. Other notable events include the Rijeka International Boat Show in September, the Porto Etno World Music Festival in July, and the Rijeka Summer Nights festival, which takes place throughout the summer and features concerts, theater performances, and more.

CONCLUSION

Rijeka may not be as well-known as other Croatian cities, but it's a hidden gem that's well worth exploring. With its historic center, vibrant culture, and delicious cuisine, Rijeka offers a unique travel experience that's sure to leave a lasting impression. So why not add it to your travel itinerary and discover this best-kept secret for yourself?

END

Printed in Great Britain
by Amazon